D1289649

FAITH AND FREEDOM

TOWARD A THEOLOGY OF LIBERATION

Revised and Enlarged Edition

ST. FRANCIS SEMINARY
SALZMANN
LIBRARY
Milwaukee, Wis. 53207

WITHDRAWN

BT
83.57
.O36
1983

FAITH AND FREEDOM

TOWARD A THEOLOGY OF LIBERATION

Revised and Enlarged Edition

Schubert M. Ogden

ABINGDON PRESS
Nashville, Tennessee

FAITH AND FREEDOM:
TOWARD A THEOLOGY OF LIBERATION
Revised and Enlarged Edition

Copyright © 1979, 1989 by Schubert M. Ogden

All rights reserved.
No part of this work may be reproduced or transmitted
in any form or by any means, electronic or mechanical,
including photocopying and recording, or by any in-
formation storage or retrieval system, except as may be
expressly permitted by the 1976 Copyright Act or in
writing from the publisher. Requests for permission
should be addressed in writing to Abingdon Press, 201
Eighth Avenue, South, Nashville, TN 37202, U.S.A.

Library of Congress Cataloging-in-Publication Data

Ogden, Schubert Miles, 1928-
    Faith and freedom: toward a theology of liberation /
Schubert Ogden — Rev. ed.
        p.   cm.
    Bibliography: p.
    ISBN 0-687-12591-X (lib. bdg, : alk. paper)
    1. Liberation theology.   2. Freedom (Theology)
    I. Title.
BT83.57.O36   1989   230--dc19   88-31540

ISBN 0-687-12591-X

Printed in the United States of America
on acid-free paper

To
The Lay Theologians
both within and without the churches
who have worked with me
at the theological task

I cannot separate the idea of deliverance from the idea of God, or even think of man as blessed except as he enters into God's redeeming purpose and labours to make others free.

— Frederick Denison Maurice

CONTENTS

PREFACE

Like the first edition of which it is a revision and enlargement, this book seeks to contribute to the ongoing discussion opened up by the various theologies of liberation. It does this by addressing the basic questions of whether and how specifically Christian faith in God and the contemporary concern for human freedom can be so understood as to interpret one another. It is also like the earlier edition, however, in being written primarily for lay rather than professional theologians who have sensed the importance of these questions to the witness of the church in our time. I continue to be impressed by the number and quality of such laypersons both within and without the churches and by the validity of their claim for help from professional theologians like myself.

As for the differences of the new edition, two seem worthy of special comment. Beyond the stylistic improvements and revisions of terminology allowed for by resetting the pages, it has enabled me, above all, to overcome the handicap of using gender-specific pronouns in referring to God. I should like to think that at least some of the readers who were understandably put off by my earlier usage will see in this difference yet another of the "subtler forms" of emancipation that theology itself not only must but also can undergo on its way toward a theology of liberation. The other main difference is the addition of a wholly new chapter 4, in which the Christology of liberation that was merely presupposed or implied by the first edition is now explicitly formulated. My hope is that, by this enlargement of the central chapters in the book, the outlines of the understanding of faith and freedom that I take to be fundamental to any adequate theology of liberation can now be more fully discerned.

This preface is not the place to reply to the criticisms of the first edition that have been made by my professional colleagues. But readers may find it helpful if I say just a word about three points in my argument where there has proved to be more than the usual amount of misunderstanding.

The first is the intention expressed by the subtitle of the book. Some reviewers of the first edition, remarking on the divergences of my positions from those typically taken by theologians of liberation, have objected that the movement of my argument is rather *away from* a theology of liberation than *toward* it. The misunderstanding here is that I do not identify, but rather distinguish, any theology of liberation toward which I intend to move and any and all theologies of liberation already on the scene. As significant as these theologies seem to me to have been in challenging all of us to develop an adequate theology of liberation, I take the actual development of such a theology to be a task for the present and future rather than an accomplishment of the past. Thus I argue that the first thing to be done toward accomplishing this task is to work out the fundamental understanding of faith and freedom that any adequate theology of liberation would have to presuppose; and I caution that the most that can be reasonably attempted in this book is to take some of the first crucial steps toward achieving such an understanding.

The second point where there has been considerable misunderstanding is what comes as close as anything to being the single thesis of the book — namely, my claim that the one process of liberation whose sole ultimate ground is the liberating love of God comprises the two quite different, although closely related, processes that I distinguish respectively as redemption and emancipation. Here the misunderstanding has typically arisen from focusing on my insistence that these two processes *must always be distinguished*, while ignoring my insistence — no less express or emphatic — that they *can never be separated*. The result is that I have often been mistaken to affirm or imply the very dualism that I have taken the greatest pains to avoid, while also avoiding the kind of monism for which "liberation" is used globally and without discrimination, as though "redemption" and "emancipation" were simply two different words for one and the same process of divine-human co-operation. There is an old saying, often cited by Protestant theologians, that one teaches well who distinguishes well. I trust that my work gives evidence that I deeply believe in the truth of this saying. But if what I do and do not take it to imply is not to be seriously misunderstood, the first distinction that readers will need to keep in mind is that between *distinguishing* things and *separating* them. As often as I may be found doing the first, I sincerely question whether I can ever be found doing the second. In any event, the whole point of my distinction between redemption and emancipation is to avoid the false choice of either simply identifying them or simply separating them by making as clear as possible exact-

ly how they are related in the one process of liberation that is grounded in God's love.

The same may be said, *mutatis mutandis,* of the
other distinction in the book that has been the third
point of widespread misunderstanding — namely,
that between witness and theology. Here, too, things
that I am concerned to distinguish some readers have
mistakenly supposed I want to separate. But in my
view, it is one and the same process of rationality that
comprises the two distinct but inseparable processes
of making or implying claims to validity, on the one
hand, and critically reflecting on the validity of such
claims, on the other. Insofar, then, as Christians bear
witness to their faith by all that they think, say, or do,
they exhibit a special form of the first kind of rational process whereby one makes or implies certain
claims to validity. Specifically, they claim that the witness they bear is both appropriate to Jesus Christ and
credible to human existence. To the extent, then, that
they critically reflect on the validity of these same
claims, they are engaged in the special form of the
second kind of rational process that I distinguish as
properly theology. Thus, as I in fact make it, the distinction between witness and theology is so far from
being or implying anything like a dualism of praxis
and theory as to be simply a special case of the general
distinction, familiar to all of us, between making or
implying validity claims, on the one hand, and critically reflecting on their validity, on the other.

There remains the happy task of expressing my
thanks to all who have made this new edition of the
book possible. To Abingdon Press, and especially to
Davis Perkins, I am particularly grateful for their will-
ingness to reissue the book and for the freedom they
have given me to revise and enlarge it. The work of
revision was considerably lightened by the proofs

provided by Angelika Fisher, editorial eecretary of the Press. And I am indebted once again to my secretary, Betty Manning, for preparing the final copy.

S.M.O.
Rollinsville, Colorado

CHAPTER 1

The Challenge of the Theologies of Liberation

Taken literally and strictly "theology" means *logos* about *theos*, or thought and speech about God. This would seem to indicate that the primary issue for theology at any time must be the issue of God. Certainly, so far as Christian theology is concerned, its first task now and always must be to understand the mystery encompassing our existence to be none other than the God and Father of our Lord Jesus Christ. But it is arguable that, in our own time and for the foreseeable future, the task of thus understanding our existence as encompassed by the reality of God is peculiarly determined by the growing concern for human liberation. This means that if the Christian witness to God is to be understood by persons today, the basic human question to which it must be presented as the answer is the question of liberation — the question as to the real nature of human freedom and its necessary ground. Insofar, then, as theology must always struggle for an understanding of God that is not only appropriate to the Christian witness but also credible to human existence, the issue with which theology today and tomorrow must above all be concerned is precisely the issue of faith and freedom — of understanding how faith in the God whom we encounter decisively through Jesus Christ is itself the answer to the question of human liberation. Such, at any rate, is the rationale for the present discussion, which is an attempt to come to terms with this issue.

Of course, there is nothing new about the conception of theology's task that I am taking for granted. And it may be helpful in understanding what I am about if we recall the course of development leading up to our present theological situation. I refer to what, speaking broadly, one may call the development of revisionary theology.

The origins of revisionary theology lie in the realization at roughly the end of the eighteenth century that neither the settled orthodoxy of the past nor the then emerging secularism represented a tenable position for Christian theology. With the rise of modern science and the growth of technology, as well as the gradual dawning of historical consciousness, the situation of Western humanity had more and more come to be determined by the new scientific picture of the world and by the resolve of men and women to assume responsibility for their own destinies — using their increasing knowledge and skill to reshape their environment, their society, and themselves. But considering that Christian orthodoxy represented, in effect, a settlement with a prescientific picture of the world, as well as a premodern assessment of the limits of human power and responsibility, one realizes at once why orthodoxy was fundamentally in conflict with the emerging secular self-understanding. Just as clear, however, is why there was an equally basic conflict between Christian faith in God as the primal source and final end of human existence and the kind of secularism for which

this world is the only world there is and our liberation of ourselves through historical progress is the
only liberation. Thus revisionary theology emerged
as an attempt by Christian thinkers to bring about a
double rapprochement: from the side of a traditional interpretation of the Christian witness toward the
modern secular world; and from a wholly secularis-
tic interpretation of modern secularity toward the essential claims of Christian faith.

Such was the project of revisionary theology as it
was carried out, first of all, in the Protestant liberal
theology of the nineteenth century, by figures like
Friedrich Schleiermacher and Albrecht Ritschl and
then later on, in Roman Catholic theology, by the so-
called Modernists. Notoriously, the main criticism
that came to be made of liberal theology was that its
attempted reinterpretation of the Christian witness
in the terms of modernity resulted in uncritically accommodating this witness to the very different claims
of modern secular culture. Yet, significantly, the
bearers of this criticism were themselves the heirs of
liberal theology, so that it was, in effect, a *self*-criticism.
What has commonly been spoken of as neo-orthodoxy
— in Protestant theology during the period between
the two world wars in the work of theologians like
Karl Barth and Reinhold Niebuhr, and in Catholic
theology somewhat later in the work of theologians
like Karl Rahner and Bernard Lonergan — is best
understood as the self-critical phase of revisionary
theology's continuing development, although there
is no denying that there were also reactionary tendencies that avoided uncritically accommodating the
witness of faith to the claims of the present only by
uncritically preserving the forms of the past.

During the 1950s, however, there were clear signs
that theology was moving once again — this time into

a genuinely postliberal phase. By this I mean a phase
in which the original revisionary strategy of double
rapprochement, as distinct from modernist accommodation, on the one hand, and fundamentalist
preservation, on the other, would determine the
shape of theological reflection. Again, speaking
broadly, one may say that this is the phase associated
with the names of Rudolf Bultmann and Paul Tillich
in Protestant theology, and Hans Küng and Edward
Schillebeeckx in Catholic Theology. But here, too,
there were unmistakable tendencies toward certain
excesses — in this case, toward the out-and-out
secularism of the death-of-God theology and associated forms of extreme accommodation to the spirit
of the times. It seems fair to say that, at the moment,
most theologians have turned their backs on all ex-
tremism — in the one direction as well as in the other
— and are exploring ways of carrying forward the essential revisionary project: a Christian theology that
will be, as I like to put it, both appropriate to the
Christian witness as it has been handed down to us
from the past and credible to human existence as it
has been given to us to live and reflect on in the
present.

There is not the least doubt in my mind that it is
this overall development of revisionary theology, including the genuinely postliberal phase in which it
now finds itself, that bears whatever promise there is
for the future of Christian theology. Just as certain
to me, however, is that what are now commonly called
theologies of liberation, which is to say, black theology and the various other ethnic theologies, women's
theology, and the theologies of the Third World, all
belong to this same course of development. They are
all examples of a revisionary type of Christian theology. But to grasp the distinctiveness of these libera-

tion theologies, over against other contemporary examples of the same theological type, it is necessary to recall an important subphase within the larger development of revisionary theology that we have just traced — namely, what is usually called "social Christianity," or the "social gospel."

As we have seen, one of the factors of modern secularity, and hence of revisionary theology from early on, was a growing historical consciousness, a consciousness that human existence in all its aspects and phases is the process by which men and women make themselves by making their own societies and cultures. Thus existing forms of government, for example, are neither divinely ordained nor naturally given but are historical products of the decisions of men and women in times past as to how their lives should be governed. This is the truth on which Thomas Paine was so insistent at the time of the American Revolution, when he argued that "although [kings] are beings of our own creating, they know not us, and are become the gods of their creators."[1] By tracing monarchy to its origins in history, Paine exposed it as an all too human institution, with the implication that what human beings had created they could also change. And so he spread the revolutionary insight that forms of government, being historical in origin, are and must be open to revision insofar as they fail to fulfill their proper function of promoting the well-being of those whose lives they govern. In this way, with the emergence of historical consciousness came the ever-clearer realization that to be fully human is to be an active *subject* of histori-

1. Thomas Paine, *Common Sense and Other Political Writings*, ed. Nelson F. Adkins (Indianapolis: Bobbs-Merrill, 1953), p. 45.

cal change, not merely its passive *object*. The clearer
this realization became, however, the clearer it also
became that most human beings, in most of the important aspects of their lives, neither are nor can be
the active subjects of their history. To continue with
our same example of forms of government, it became
obvious that, in most cases, the decisions by which
these forms have been produced have not been the
decisions of all whose lives they governed but only of
some, the privileged few by whom the fate of the
many is by and large determined.

This recognition of fundamental human inequality and injustice, which seemed all the more intoler-
able the more the already privileged classes proved
to be the principal beneficiaries of modern progress,
is what gave rise around the middle of the nineteenth
century to the movement of social Christianity, or the
social gospel. Because the scope of human power and
responsibility includes, in principle, the whole social
and cultural order, the love for our neighbors as ourselves entailed by faith in the gospel lays upon every
Christian responsibility for fundamental change in
society and culture themselves — for such structural
or systemic change as may be necessary to overcome
the inequality and injustice of the existing order. Ever
since its emergence, this essential insight of the social gospel has continued to be an important in-
gredient of revisionary theology, even if individual
revisionary theologies have at times been less concerned with practical issues of action and justice than
with more theoretical questions of belief and truth.

It is clearly in the tradition of this same insight
that the various theologies of liberation today are to
be located, their distinctiveness as revisionary theologies lying precisely in their intense preoccupation
with the issues of action and justice. Yet it would be

a mistake, in my opinion, to see the theologies of liberation as nothing more than a contemporary re-expression of the social gospel. For there is at least this important difference: whereas the social gospel, after all, was typically a movement from within the relatively advantaged human group to take account of the differing historical situations and needs of persons belonging to disadvantaged groups, the theologies of liberation are typically movements within the disadvantaged groups themselves to provide a theological self-interpretation of their own situations and needs. The observation has often been made that it is only after a certain amount of relevant historical progress has already been made by a group that it begins to lay claim to power. The emergence in recent years of the various theologies of liberation — whether black theology, or women's theology, or Third World theology — confirms the soundness of this observation. For these theologies have emerged within the various groups of whose situations and needs they are an attempt at theological interpretation only after these groups have already progressed sufficiently to be more than the passive victims of historical fate. In this connection, the statement of James H. Cone is revealing: "Black theology is the theological arm of Black Power, and Black Power is the political arm of Black Theology."[2]

This must suffice as a historical introduction to the conception of theology's task that I am here assuming. In all essentials, I have argued, it is the same conception that has been determinative for the whole development of revisionary theology from its liberal

2. James H. Cone, "Black Power, Black Theology, and the Study of Theology and Ethics," *Theological Education*, 6 (1970): 209.

beginnings right up to our present postliberal situation. I trust it has now also become clear why, in my view, the theologies of liberation that have become so prominent on the contemporary theological scene simply cannot be ignored. As distinctive as they certainly are from other contemporary expressions of a truly revisionary theological outlook and approach, these theologies are authentic expressions of essentially the same type of Christian theology; and my conviction is that, with all their limitations, they are among the more forwardlooking and hopeful expressions of theology on the present scene.

Why a Challenge — and to Whom?

This brings us to our main topic: the challenge of the theologies of liberation. If one of the necessary conditions of something's being a challenge to someone is that it be in important respects different from anything else that one already is or has, another such condition is that there be at least some respects in which it is also the same. The preceding discussion will presumably have made clear why, so far as I am concerned, there is enough similarity between my own understanding of theology's task and that of the theologies of liberation that they can, indeed, be a challenge at least to me — provided, at any rate, that there are also some respects in which they are sufficiently different. But is there such difference? And who is it, exactly, other than myself, to whom the theologies of liberation are a challenge?

I can best answer these questions by insisting more than I yet have on the distinction I have already made between witness and theology. I began by saying that, in its strict, literal sense, "theology" means *logos* about *theos,* or thought and speech about God. But in going on, then, to talk about the task of theology, I evidently implied a stricter understanding of theology than simply thought and speech about God in general. For if the task of theology, as I argued, is so to think and speak about God as to be both appropriate to the Christian witness and credible to human existence, then there is a difference between the thought and speech about God on which theology reflects, which I speak of as Christian witness, and the thought and speech about God in which theology itself is supposed to consist. In other words, what distinguishes theology proper from the thought and speech about God that make up Christian witness generally is that theology is either the process or the product of critically reflecting on this witness with a view to satisfying the twin criteria of appropriateness and credibility.

In general, to reflect is to take something that *appears* to be the case and then to ask more or less deliberately, methodically, and in a reasoned way whether it *really* is so. Moreover, there is serious work for reflection to do whenever something is *said* to be the case. For, first of all, one must determine what is *meant* by what is said — what is meant and what is said are never quite the same — and then, secondly, one must inquire whether what is meant *really* is the case, in the sense of asserting things to be as they actually are. In saying that theology, properly speaking, is distinct from the witness of faith because it is either the process or the product of critically reflecting on this witness, I mean that theology is the kind of reflection that asks in a deliberate, methodical, and reasoned way about the meaning and truth of the Christian witness of faith.

If we think about it, we realize at once that theology thus understood as reflection on the Christian

witness so as to determine its meaning and truth is a
necessary task. To be a Christian is to be called to witness to one's faith in and for the world. But, clearly,
to determine whether one's witness is adequate, in
the sense of being both appropriate and credible, requires that one engage in theological reflection. More
than this, even to become a Christian in the first place
requires the same kind of engagement, since one cannot responsibly believe a witness of faith whose meaning one does not understand, nor can one responsibly judge a witness to be true unless one feels the force
of at least some reasons that may be given for its truth.

To recognize the necessity of theological reflection, however, is also to understand why the task of
theology is by no means the task merely of the special group of professionals commonly called theologians. Just as bearing witness to one's faith is the
responsibility of every Christian believer, to which
each of us is called by our baptism and which we each
assume for ourselves with our confirmation, so critically reflecting on the meaning and truth of the
Christian witness is also a responsibility that de-
volves upon every single one of us — and even upon
anyone who would responsibly become one of us. I
do not in the least mean by this that there are not
important differences between being the *lay* theologian to which all Christians are called and being
the *professional* theologian to which only some Christians are called, any more than I should question the
differences between the lay ministry of every Christian believer and the professional ministry of the
church's representative ministers. But, however important the differences between the lay and the professional theologian, they are not more important
than those between the lay and the professional min-
ister. The theological task of critically reflecting on

one's witness so as to determine its meaning and truth as surely belongs in some way to each of us as Christians as does the ministerial task of somehow bearing this witness by all that we say or do.

Because this is so, there is at least one important respect in which the theologies of liberation are sufficiently different to be a challenge not only to me but to any reader of this book as well. Being reflection on witness rather than witness itself, any such theology simply must be different from, even if in other respects it is the same as, the witness on which it reflects. To this extent, it cannot fail to be a challenge to anyone charged with the responsibility either of bearing the Christian witness or of seriously responding to its claims. This is particularly so because a theology as such differs from witness just insofar as, being either the process or the product of critical reflection on witness, *it has to give reasons for its assertions*. It is theology at all only because or insofar as it gives reasons for thinking that its claims are both appropriate to the Christian witness and credible to human existence. But, then, insofar as the theologies of liberation really are theologies in this sense of the word, they are unavoidably a challenge to every Christian responsible for bearing the witness of faith, as well as to any other person who is so much as concerned to understand this witness. For by giving reasons for the appropriateness and credibility of their assertions, these theologies explicitly raise the question of the adequacy of any Christian's witness, and hence are a challenge to him or her, as well as to anyone else who would responsibly decide either to accept or to reject the claim of this witness to be true.

Still, as important as it is to recognize that the theologies of liberation are and must be a challenge to every Christian believer responsible for bearing the witness of faith, this is not the only, or even the primary, respect in which I have ventured to speak of the challenge of these theologies. I maintain that they also pose a challenge to each of us because or insofar as we ourselves are theologians, who, either as laypersons or as professionals, also have the responsibility of critically reflecting on the Christian witness so as to answer the questions of its meaning and truth. Thus I have tried to make clear in the subtitle of this book that it is primarily with respect to our responsibility to work toward a *theology* of liberation that the theologies of liberation are a challenge to us. Accordingly, it is as one who is himself a theologian speaking to others who, in their ways, are also theologians that I am moved to speak of the challenge of the theologies of liberation.

The Nature of the Challenge

The question now is as to the nature of this challenge. In trying to answer it, I recall my statement about the necessary conditions of something's being a challenge to someone — namely, that it must be, in suitably different respects, both similar to and different from other things that one already is or has or does. This general rule has two corollaries that we need to keep in mind.

First, the similarity that must exist between one's own theological outlook and approach and that typical of the theologies of liberation in order for them to be a challenge need not extend as far as it happens to do in my own case. As I have explained, I myself share with these theologies the general outlook and approach of all revisionary theology, according to which there is not simply one criterion of theological adequacy but two — not simply appropriateness to the Christian witness but also credibility to human existence. Even if one does not happen to share this basic outlook and approach, however, one can still be challenged by the theologies of liberation, provided only that there is at least some respect in which one's own way of doing theology and theirs are the same. Such similarity may extend no further, say, than a shared recognition that theology, as critical reflection on witness, has to be responsible to some criterion or criteria and, consequently, must give good reasons for its assertions.

The second corollary is that the difference that must exist in order for some other theology to be a challenge to our own may take two different forms, either of which suffices to make it a challenge to us. Specifically, the theologies of liberation can be, and I believe are, a challenge to our own theological efforts both because of what they have already succeeded in doing over against our own failures and because of what they have as yet failed to do, relative, if not to our successes, then at least to our resources for doing the same thing more successfully.

The preceding discussion should have made clear what I regard as the main successes of the theologies of liberation. For one thing, they are basically committed to a revisionary theological outlook and approach; and, for another, they are intensely preoccupied within that commitment with practical issues of action and justice, as distinct from theoretical questions of belief and truth. Both of these seem to me to be profoundly challenging to much of the theology commonly done among us by professional as well as by lay theologians, just because of our own failures at one or both of these fundamental points. But even with this considerable measure of success, which alone makes them a challenge not only to me but to many others, these theologies also appear to suffer from certain typical failures that make them all the more challenging. This is because they lay upon us the responsibility of so using the resources available to us as to contribute toward overcoming their failures — and, in this way, to do our own part toward a theology of liberation. As I see it, then, the challenge presented by the various liberation theologies is that of working out a still more adequate theology of liberation than any of them has yet achieved.

To make as clear as possible just wherein this challenge seems to me to lie, I want to identify four points where, as I understand them, the theologies of liberation typically fail to carry out the theological project to which they are committed in an adequate way. I stress the word "typically," for in speaking here and elsewhere in this book of "theologies of liberation," I am speaking of particular theological efforts or positions only insofar as they conform to a certain ideal type. I am confident that there are any number of theologies on the present scene that more or less closely conform to this type, and hence could be more or less fairly characterized as "theologies of liberation." But since my purpose here is neither to characterize nor to criticize any particular theology, I make use of this phrase solely to characterize a certain way of doing theology that is more or less represented by any number of theologies but can hardly be exactly identified with any of them — not even those that have characterized themselves by use of this phrase. Moreover, I shall identify the four points where the theologies of liberation have failed by giving four reasons why I, for one, cannot ignore the challenge of trying to work toward a more adequate theology of liberation.

I cannot ignore this challenge, first of all, because *these theologies typically are not so much theology as witness.* The evidence for this is that they tend rather to be the rationalization of positions already taken than the process or the product of critical reflection on these positions. We will have occasion later, in chapter 5, to observe that much the same may be said about the long tradition of Christian theology. The vast majority of theologies have been, in effect if hardly in intention, Christian ideologies, in the precise sense of rationalizing the prior claims of the Christian witness instead of critically inquiring as to their meaning and truth. Be this as it may, it is typical of all the theologies of liberation that they tend to obscure any distinction between theology and witness — not only by what they expressly say about them but even more by what they actually do, or fail to do. Their justification for this, typically, is that theology exists, not for its own sake, but for the sake of the church's witness, its liberating praxis, which theology is supposed to serve. Hence their polemic against so-called academic theology, and their insistence that theology itself must be "engaged," and so on. But, in my view, the issue is not *whether* theology properly serves the praxis of the church as an end beyond itself; the issue, rather, is *how* theology properly performs this service. Does it do so by uncritically assuming that the claims of the Christian witness are true, or that the liberation it promises is one and the same with that for which men and women today are asking? Or is its service to the church's witness the indirect service of critically reflecting on these matters and taking pains to give good reasons for its conclusions concerning them?

I cannot ignore the challenge of the liberation theologies, in the second place, because *they typically focus on the existential meaning of God for us without dealing at all adequately with the metaphysical being of God in itself*. It is the chief defining characteristic of religion generally that, while it is neither simply a metaphysics nor simply an ethics, it is in a peculiar way both. By this I mean that a religion is at once an understanding of the ultimate reality of self, others, and the whole and an understanding of our own possibilities of existing and acting in relation to this ultimate reality. Because this is so, theology as the process or the product of critically reflecting on a religion ought ideally to reflect not just one of these two aspects but both of them. But it is a characteristic of the theologies of liberation, consistent with their typical preoccupation with practical issues of action and justice, that they are a reflection more of the ethical or existential aspect of the Christian religion than of its metaphysical aspect. In fact, they commonly display a marked impatience with the more theoretical questions of belief and truth, considered simply in themselves in their own right. Their justification for such impatience, typically, is that faith, after all, is more than merely believing certain things about God; for them, faith — being primarily trust in and loyalty to God — necessarily involves existing and acting in a certain way, as distinct from merely holding certain beliefs to be true. But, as I see it, the issue is not *whether* faith in God is primarily an existential matter; the issue, rather, is *how* theology properly takes account of this fact. Does it do so by focusing solely or primarily on the existential meaning of God for our own existence and praxis even to the point of continuing to assume certain traditional metaphysical beliefs about God uncritically? Or does it begin with faith in its existential meaning for us in order, then, to go on and make fully explicit the metaphysical beliefs about the being of God in itself that faith as such necessarily implies?

I cannot ignore the challenge to work toward a theology of liberation, in the third place, because *the liberation theologies typically tend to confuse — or do not adequately distinguish — two essentially different, though closely related, forms of liberation.* If this book has a single thesis, it is that the one process of liberation whose necessary ground is God comprises two quite different, even if closely related, processes that can and must be distinguished respectively as redemption and emancipation, God being understood correspondingly as both the Redeemer and the Emancipator. Consequently, from the standpoint of this thesis, the one thing that any adequate theology of liberation has to avoid is speaking about liberation in merely global, undiscriminating terms, thereby either confusing or failing to distinguish its two irreducibly different forms. And yet nothing is more striking about the theologies of liberation than just such global talk of liberation, with its tacit confusion of redemption with emancipation, of God the Redeemer with God the Emancipator. Indeed, concerned as they are with what they call the praxis of liberation, they are insistent that there is but one process by which human beings are freed from bondage, and they are suspicious of all the usual theological attempts to make any distinctions with respect to this process. They justify such suspicion, typically, by arguing that it is precisely as one integral witness to our own and all other men's and women's freedom from bondage that the Christian witness has been handed down to us from the apostles; and it is this freedom, accordingly, that must be the whole point of theology. But, in my view, the issue is not *whether* there is a single process of liberation that is the whole point of witness and theology; the issue, rather, is *how* theology properly understands this one process. Does it do so by taking liberation to be only or primarily the emancipation from bondage called for by the various movements for human freedom — political, economic, cultural, racial, and sexual? Or does it do so by taking liberation to be primarily the redemption from death, transience, and sin attested by the apostolic witness — and only secondarily, though necessarily, the emancipation from every other form of bondage that redemption itself makes mandatory?

I cannot ignore the challenge of the theologies of liberation, in the fourth place, because *they typically have too restricted or provincial an understanding of the various forms of bondage from which men and women, as well as their fellow creatures, need to be emancipated.* Experience enforces the insight that misery has many forms and that even the best efforts to overcome one of them may be altogether oblivious of others. Thus in a recent history of American Communism, a party wife, weary of feeding her husband's comrades, is reported to have finally exploded: "While you sit on your ass making the revolution, *I'm* out there in the kitchen like a slavey. What we need is a revolution in this *house*."[3] Yet, notwithstanding this insight, each of the theologies of liberation characteristically orients itself to but one form or another of human bondage — political, economic, cultural, racial, or sexual — as though freedom from it were the whole of emancipation. Their justification for this, typically, is that

3. Vivian Gornick, *The Romance of American Communism* (New York: Basic Books, 1978); quoted in *Time*, February 6 (1978): 90.

bondage, like freedom, is never to be found merely in general but always and only in just such concrete forms, from which those who suffer the bondage have the right to be freed, even as those of us who can do so have the responsibility of working for their emancipation. But, as I see it, the issue is not *whether* each of these forms of bondage, as well as all of them together, is exactly that; the issue, rather, is *how* theology understands this to be the case. Does it do so by supposing that some of them, or all of them together, are *the* bondage that makes emancipation imperative? Or does it try to keep in mind the necessarily multiple forms of bondage, as well as the presence of yet subtler forms than those that most obviously claim our attention and action?

These reasons seem to be more than sufficient to explain why the project of a theology of liberation is the challenge put to the rest of us by the already existing theologies that bear this name. If this implies that these theologies have not wholly succeeded in what they themselves have projected — for at least the reasons I have given — it also implies that the project itself is a challenge to the best we have to offer as theologians. The task before us, therefore, is to join in the project and to make our own contribution to it — confident not only that there is room for anything we have to contribute, but also that the intrinsic worth of the project will justify even the most modest contribution we can offer.

In taking up this challenge, as I propose to do in the chapters that follow, I would underscore the indications already given that our task here is limited to moving *toward* a theology of liberation and that taking a few important steps in this direction is all we can hope to do. My comments just now about the necessarily multiple forms of bondage and the

presence of subtler forms than we commonly recognize will have made clear that I envisage the possibility of other, rather different theologies of liberation from those that already exist. But it should also
have become clear that any such theology would not
be *the*, but only *a* theology of liberation. There would
still be room, just as there is now, for many other such
theologies. Nevertheless, it seems to me that any
theology of liberation that were at all adequate would
share with every other in the same fundamental understanding of faith in God, given the basic human
question of freedom. Consequently, our most urgent
theological task, as I see it, is to clarify just this fundamental theological understanding. It is to this important, even if limited, task that the succeeding
chapters are devoted.

CHAPTER 2

Faith as the Existence of Freedom: In Freedom and for Freedom

The challenge of the theologies of liberation, I have argued, is to join them in working toward a still more adequate understanding of faith and freedom than any of them has already managed to achieve. Such a project remains to be carried out because, for various reasons, the existing liberation theologies typically have not yet succeeded in realizing it. Thus, whether because they are not so much theology as witness, or because they stress the meaning of God for us without dealing adequately with the being of God in itself, or because they tend to confuse the liberation that is redemption with the liberation that is emancipation, or finally because they have too provincial an understanding of the forms of bondage from which some or all of us need to be emancipated — whether for one or more of these reasons, the liberation theologies already on the scene have typically failed to develop the kind of theology of liberation that is clearly indicated.

In now taking up their challenge to contribute toward such a theology, I shall be concerned, especially in this chapter and the next, with what I have called the fundamental theological understanding that any adequate theology of liberation would perforce share with every other. Specifically, I shall be concerned with clarifying the essential meaning of Christian faith in God, assuming that the question in terms of which such faith is to be understood is the question asked by men and women today concerning the nature and ground of human freedom.

Two further comments are necessary to introduce the argument of these chapters.

It should be evident by now that, as I view the task of Christian theology, the first concern of the theologian must always be to achieve a reflective understanding of the Christian witness that is appropriate to this witness itself. But this obviously raises the question of how the criterion of appropriateness thus acknowledged is actually to be applied. How, exactly, does one go about determining what is and is not appropriate theology? What is the standard or norm of such appropriateness?

Historically, Protestant theology has replied to this question by pointing to Scripture, especially the New Testament. Although Protestants have been clear right from the beginning that the sole ultimate source of theological authority is Jesus Christ himself, who, as Luther liked to say, is "king of Scripture" (*rex scripturae*), they have also been insistent that the Christ who is, indeed, king even of Scripture can be none other than the Christ of whom Scripture alone is the primary witness.[1] It is in this sense that they have traditionally upheld the principle "Scripture *alone*" (*sola scriptura*), as over against the traditional Roman Catholic appeal to "Scripture *and* tradition," which is

---

1. *Luther's Works*, Vol. 26, ed. Jaroslav Pelikan (St. Louis: Concordia Publishing House, 1963), p. 295.

to say, Scripture and the *magisterium*, or teaching office of the church, epitomized in the infallible teaching office of the Pope. But one of the consequences of the historical-critical study of Scripture, which is perhaps the greatest single achievement of revisionary theology, is the recognition that even the writings that comprise the canon of the New Testament are not original witness to Christ, and hence not properly apostolic. On the contrary, because they all evidently make use of sources earlier than themselves, they are all more or less later interpretations of the apostolic witness, which was historically prior to them and must now be reconstructed from them. In other words, the historic Protestant insistence on Scripture alone as primary norm over against all tradition has now become untenable because the writings of Scripture themselves are now known to be — precisely tradition!

I do not mention this important consequence of scriptural study in order to go into all the difficulties it raises, much less to try to deal with them. But it has seemed to me of some importance to explain why I myself am no longer able to give the reply to the question of the standard or norm of theological appropriateness that Protestant theologians have traditionally given. Were I to give adequate reasons for thinking that the assertions I shall make about faith and freedom are, in fact, appropriate to the Christian witness, I should feel bound to appeal not simply to Scripture, or even to the New Testament, but to what I understand to be the true apostolic and, therefore, canonical witness. I refer to the earliest layer of witness now accessible to us through historical-critical study of the synoptic Gospels, which, following one of the most careful students of this whole matter,

Willi Marxsen, I call the "Jesus-kerygma."[2] Ever since
the canon of Scripture was gradually decided by the
early church, the true standard or norm of canonicity,
and hence of all Christian witness and theology, has
been the witness of the apostles, in the sense of the
original witness to Jesus as the Christ upon which all
other Christian witness and theology, as well as all
Christian faith, necessarily depend. But if we today,
given our own historical methods and knowledge, are
to continue to submit our assertions to this same
standard or norm, we have no choice but to locate it,
not in the New Testament writings as we now have
them, but in this earliest kerygma, or witness to Jesus,
that we are now able to reconstruct by critical study
of the Gospels. Consequently, even though I shall not
be able to show at all adequately how the assertions I
shall make do, in fact, measure up to this norm, it is
on the basis of my continuing study of the Jesus-
kerygma that I shall be making these assertions, and
it is precisely to it, as the true Christian canon, that I
should feel obliged to appeal, finally, in giving
reasons for them.

The other introductory comment I have to make
is by way of explaining the rationale of this and the
following chapter. I have argued that theologians
today are called to work out a theology of liberation
because or insofar as it is in terms of the question of
freedom that men and women today typically ask the
existential question concerning the ultimate meaning of their existence. Behind this argument is my
assumption that it is precisely this existential question, whether in terms of freedom or some other

2.   Willi Marxsen, *The New Testament as the Church's Book*,
trans. James E. Mignard (Philadelphia: Fortress Press, 1972),
pp. 64-128.

terms, that is the religious and, therefore, theological question. Implied by this assumption is that religious assertions generally, and, consequently, the assertions of Christian witness and theology in particular, are existential assertions. Whatever else they may be about, they are always concerned with our own possibilities of existing and acting in the world, and hence give answer in some way or other to this existential question.

To be sure, I have already said enough in criticizing the theologies of liberation to make clear why no theology can legitimately focus solely on the existential meaning of God for us, to the exclusion of all considerations of the metaphysical being of God in itself. Not only the Christian religion but any religion has by its very nature a metaphysical as well as an existential aspect. Consequently, if religious assertions are always about our own possibilities of existing and acting, and are to that extent existential, they are also always about the ultimate reality apart from which we could neither exist nor act at all, and so are also metaphysical. In fact, the most careful analyses of religious language by both social scientists and philosophers have again and again confirmed that the chief defining characteristic of a religious assertion is that it is about our own existence in the world only in relation to the strictly ultimate reality that is its primal source and final end — and vice versa.

Because this is so, theological reflection on religious assertions — or in the case of Christian theology, on the assertions comprising the Christian witness of faith — can assume no other form than an explication of the existential meaning of God for us as both implying and implied by an explication of the metaphysical being of God in itself. It is just because, on the basis of the apostolic witness, we under-

stand the whole of reality encompassing our existence to be in itself the God whom Jesus represents as
Father that we both can and should understand ourselves in the world in the distinctive way in which
this witness summons us to do. But the converse statement is also true: it is just because, on the basis of
the same apostolic witness, we both can and should
understand our existence in the world in this distinctive way that we must understand the primal source
and final end of our existence to be none other than
the God and Father of Jesus Christ.

This is the reason, then, for the structure and
movement of the argument in this chapter and the
next, which are devoted respectively to these two
mutually dependent explications: of the meaning of
God for us, and of the being of God in itself. Accordingly, what is said in either chapter can be rightly understood only by taking account of what is also said
in the other. At the same time, I would insist that the
order of the two explications is by no means arbitrary,
since there are the best of reasons in the very nature
of faith itself for beginning with the existential meaning of God for us before going on to explicate the
metaphysical being of God in itself.

Faith as Existence *in* Freedom

Our first question, then, is about the existential
meaning of faith in God, given the contemporary concern for human freedom. The answer I shall give to
this question is the one summarized in the title of
this chapter: faith is the existence of freedom. By this
I mean, quite simply, that the distinctive way of understanding ourselves in the world that is properly
described as Christian faith in God is a way of exist-

ing and acting *in* freedom and *for* it. This answer must now be unpacked, and I begin with the first assertion it involves, that faith in God is existence *in* freedom.

No doubt the principal difficulty in accepting, if not, indeed, in understanding, this assertion is the long-standing and widespread tendency within the church and without it to identify faith with belief, or more accurately, with *belief about*, as distinct from *belief in*. This tendency is evident from a very early time in the life of the church, as is clear from the polemical claim of the Letter of James in the New Testament that "faith apart from works is dead" (2:26). As every good Protestant is aware, this claim has always been a problem, since it seems so obviously to conflict with the characteristic claim of Paul that "a man is justified by faith alone apart from works of the law" (Rom 3:28). But one of the results of the continuing historical-critical study of Scripture is the conviction, now widely shared by New Testament scholars, that James' polemic is not really directed against Paul's own understanding of faith and justification but, rather, against a very different understanding of faith, according to which it means believing certain things about God, in the sense of sincerely holding them to be true. For Paul himself, on the contrary, faith is understood primarily as obedient submission to the gift and demand of God's grace, and hence as belief in God itself, in the twofold sense of trust in God's love and loyalty to its cause. Thus the only faith that Paul understands to be a justifying faith is not the mere belief *about* God that James has in mind when he hears the word "faith," but, rather, that belief *in* God that, as Paul himself puts it, is always and of necessity "faith working through love" (Gal 5:6).

Far from conflicting with Paul's view, then, James' insistence that works are necessary to justification is

by way of making the very point that Paul himself
would undoubtedly have wanted to make, had he assumed James' different understanding of faith as
mere belief *about* God, instead of what he in fact does
assume, namely, that faith is primarily belief *in* God
and hence fidelity to God's love as well as confidence
in it. (It seems worth remarking in passing that it is
from just this sort of example that one can learn from
the New Testament itself that the church's teachers
and theologians have always recognized that making
statements appropriate to what the apostolic witness
means is something different and more demanding
than merely repeating what it *says*. James would certainly have done far worse a job in bearing the witness of faith than he did if he had continued to use
Paul's words in a situation in which they could no
longer be understood to mean what Paul himself
meant by them.)

This tendency, already evident in the New Testament, to interpret faith as only, or primarily, a matter of believing certain things to be true, was all the
more strongly reinforced the more the church moved
out of its original Jewish environment and sought to
understand its witness in a Hellenistic religious and
cultural context. Indeed, the classic definitions of
"faith" in patristic and medieval theology make clear
that this is the interpretation of faith that increasingly came to prevail in the church. Nor was the
Reformers' vigorous attempt to reintroduce the earlier and more scriptural understanding of faith as
belief in God, and hence as trust in God's love and
loyalty to God, sufficient to keep even the Protestant
churches and theology from once again succumbing
to the same tendency. Consequently, right up to today,
persons both within the church and without it commonly understand the faith in God to which the

Christian witness is the summons as primarily, if not only, a matter of believing certain things about God — namely, those things that they understand to comprise proper Christian belief, whether orthodox or otherwise.

As long as this common understanding of faith prevails, my assertion that faith in God is existence in freedom is not likely to seem true. For that matter, it will hardly even be understood. Nevertheless, there are few things a theologian can say more confidently than that the understanding of faith as primarily belief about God has no warrant whatever either in Scripture or, more importantly, in the apostolic witness that is the norm even of the claims of Scripture. Just when one orients oneself to theology's primary source in Scripture and to its apostolic norm, it becomes clear beyond any question that Christian faith in God, in its primary sense, is an existential matter of believing *in* God, as distinct from an intellectual matter of believing certain things *about* God.

It is true that this primary sense of "faith" is not its only sense — not even in Scripture or in the witness of the apostles — and that the distinction on which I have insisted between belief in God and belief about God ought never to be construed as implying their separation. Contrary to David Hume, not everything that can be distinguished can be separated, and this is nowhere more obvious, or important, than in this matter of the two senses of "faith." To trust in God's love as it is decisively re-presented to us through Jesus Christ, or to be loyal to God's love by loving God and, in God, all whom God loves, is clearly to presuppose that the mysterious whole encompassing our existence really is the God who, quite apart from our own trust and loyalty, loves both us and all our fellow creatures. Consequently, unless these beliefs about God were true — unless strictly ultimate reality really were the God of all-embracing love — there clearly would be no point whatever either in our trusting in God's love or in our being faithful to God. Even so, the inseparability of belief *in* God from belief *about* God should in no way obscure the fact that the first is the primary sense of "faith" in the normative witness of the apostles, as well as in Scripture generally. The justifying faith in God attested by Paul and rediscovered by the Reformers is, first of all, trust in the promise of God's love declared to us through Jesus Christ and loyalty to the cause of God's love that all things be brought to their proper fulfillment, to God's glory.

It is to faith thus understood, then, that my assertion is intended to refer when I say that faith in God is existence *in* freedom. And the reason for this assertion, as what I have already said will have indicated, is this: according to normative Christian witness, the mysterious whole encompassing our existence as its primal source and final end, whence it comes and whither it goes, is none other than God — specifically, the God and Father of our Lord Jesus Christ, who is the pure, unbounded love of all things and the Father of every man and woman. Because it is in this God's all-embracing love that all things have their beginning and end, and because there is nothing whatever that can separate us from God's love — not even death and transience, or our own sinful forgetfulness of its presence — because it is this love that ever was, is, and remains our only final end, even as it is our only primal source, we are one and all presented in every moment of our lives with the gift and demand of faith. This is to say that we are continually presented with the gift and demand of utterly trusting in God's love as the only ultimate ground of our own being and meaning, as well as of the being and meaning of everything else, and of being utterly loyal to this same love as the only cause inclusive enough in its concern for the fulfillment of all things to claim all our love and service.

Of course, the gift and demand of faith in God are decisively *re*-presented to us through Jesus Christ as we encounter him through the Christian witness of faith. As we shall see in chapter 4, what we as Christians mean by "Jesus Christ" is the event in our common human history that is both the origin and the principle of our own faith in God and witness to him and is originally attested as such in the normative witness of the apostles. This means that the Jesus to whom we bear witness as the Christ is the decisive re-presentation, or presenting again through concepts and symbols, of the same gift and demand of faith in God that are present in our actual existence as soon and as long as we exist and act humanly at all. Conversely, it means that the possibility of faith in God implicitly presented to each of us in our actual existence is none other than the possibility of faith in God explicitly re-presented to all of us through Jesus Christ.

But faith understood as an existence in utter trust in God's love and utter loyalty to God's cause as they are decisively revealed in Christ can only be an existence in freedom — and that in two distinct, albeit closely related senses of the word.

Faith is existence in freedom, in the first place, in the negative sense of *freedom from* — freedom *from* all things, ourselves and the world, as in any way essential to determining the ultimate meaning of our lives. Because faith, as we have seen, is, first of all, utter trust in the love of God as the primal source and the final end of our own unique existence, as

well as of everything else, to exist in faith is to be
freed from any compulsion to find the ultimate
ground of one's life in something else alongside God.
Being bound utterly and completely to God, the
believer is utterly and completely freed from everything else. Indeed, the believer exists in the
knowledge that, no matter what happens, good or
bad, it is finally indifferent or of no consequence insofar as we always exist under God's loving care and,
together with all our fellow creatures, are finally safe
— in the sense that our lives, like theirs, are embraced
within God's boundless and everlasting love, where
they have an abiding meaning in spite of our own
death and sin and the transience of all things. Because the mystery encompassing our existence is the
limitless acceptance of God's love, faith as the acceptance of this acceptance, and, in this sense, as trust
in God's love, is existence in freedom *from* literally
everything else.

For the very same reason, faith is existence in
freedom, in the second place, in the positive sense of
freedom for — freedom *for* literally everything else,
ourselves and the world, as all worthy of our own
love and devoted service. Just because faith is, first
of all, utter trust in God's love for us, to exist in faith
is to be freed from ourselves and the world and, at
one and the same time, also to be freed for them. It
is existence in freedom in this second or positive sense
that is actualized by our faith insofar as it is not only
trust in God's love but also loyalty to God and, therefore, also to all those to whom God is loyal — which
means, of course, literally everyone. Thus, being
bound utterly and completely to God, the believer is
utterly and completely freed for everything else. Indeed, the believer exists in the knowledge that all
that happens, good or bad, is so far from being indif-

ferent or of no consequence as to give concrete content or direction to our own responsibility to care — to care for all those who are or become our neighbors and, by serving their creaturely needs, to optimize the limits of their freedom to become fully themselves. Because the mystery encompassing our lives is God's boundless acceptance, faith as the trusting acceptance of this acceptance is also the freedom to accept all those whom God accepts and, therefore, is existence in freedom *for* all things, our fellow creatures as well as ourselves.

Faith as Existence *for* Freedom

This understanding of faith as existence in freedom, in the positive sense of freedom *for* ourselves and the world, as well as in the negative sense of freedom *from* them, is nothing new in Christian theology. As a matter of fact, to this extent, there has been an explicit theology of liberation ever since the New Testament; for it is in these very terms, of freedom from and freedom for all things, that Paul, notably, explicates the whole meaning of existence in faith — making use of the Stoic concept of "freedom" (*eleutheria*), which, having no precedent in the Old Testament and Judaism, allowed for a novel theological explication of the meaning of faith in God. Thus Paul can write to the Corinthians, "Now the Lord is the Spirit, and where the Spirit of the Lord is, there is freedom" (2 Cor 3:17), just as he can attest to the Galatians, "For freedom Christ has set us free; stand fast therefore, and do not submit again to a yoke of bondage" (Gal 5:1). Not surprisingly, the Protestant Reformers, who were so extensively dependent on Paul, characteristically interpreted Christian exis-

tence precisely as existence in freedom — the classic
of all such interpretations being Luther's treatise, *The
Freedom of a Christian*, in which he summarizes all that
it means to be a Christian in the two paradoxical statements: "A Christian is a perfectly free lord of all, subject to none," and "A Christian is a perfectly dutiful
servant of all, subject to everyone."[3]

This second statement that the Christian who exists in perfect freedom is at the same time a dutiful
servant, bound to the service of everyone, already
opens up the other thing we must consider in this
chapter. It is Luther himself whose support I can
claim in making the second assertion implied by my
title — namely, that faith is also existence *for* freedom.
In making this assertion, I particularly have in mind
another statement of Luther's, to the effect that "the
first and highest work of love that a Christian ought
to do once he has come to believe is that he should
bring others to faith even as he himself has come to
it."[4] Luther's point is obvious enough: to exist in faith
is to do the works of love; and the first and highest
of such works is to open up for others, also, the possibility of existing in faith. But if we now reflect on
this point in the light of the conclusion we have just
reached, that the possibility of existing in faith can
be nothing other than the possibility of existing in
freedom, in freedom *from* all things and in freedom
for them, then the force of Luther's point, clearly, is

3. *Luther's Works*, Vol. 31, ed. Harold J. Grimm
(Philadelphia: Muhlenberg Press, 1957), p. 344.
4. I have never been able to locate the exact source of
this quotation, which hung as a motto over the desk of my
teacher, Joachim Wach. But Luther often makes the same
point, as, e.g., in *Luther's Works*, Vol. 30, ed. Jaroslav Pelikan
(St. Louis: Concordia Publishing House, 1967), p. 33.

that the faith that is existence *in* freedom is, by its very nature, also existence *for* freedom — for the freedom of all the others, for whom the Christian is freed to live through utterly trusting in God's love.

We may be quite sure that what Luther had in mind in saying that the first and highest work of love is to bring others to faith even as we ourselves have come to it is that the Christian's preeminent responsibility is to bear witness to the grace of God in Jesus Christ. Certainly, in Luther's view, the only one who can bring any person to faith in the strict sense of the words is God as God encounters us through Christ, in the Holy Spirit. For it is God's prevenient grace of accepting our lives into God's own that is the necessary condition of the possibility of our accepting God's acceptance through faith. Therefore, the only way in which we as Christians could possibly bring others to faith is to bear witness to them of God's redeeming love, which must itself be the only ultimate ground of their faith even as it is of ours. What Luther's point comes to, then, is that the first and highest work of any Christian who exists in freedom is to bear witness to others of the boundless love of God, whose meaning for them is the gift and demand of the same radical freedom.

This raises the question of just how the Christian is to bear such witness. Ordinarily, the term "witness" is understood in a fairly strict sense to refer to specific words and deeds having explicitly to do with the redeeming love of God through Jesus Christ. Thus the paradigms of witness are all assumed to be specifically religious, being, first of all, the church's explicit proclamation of Christ through its preaching and sacraments and, dependent thereon, the explicit testimony of individual Christians to God's redeeming love. But while this assumption certainly is under-

standable, it is mistaken, in my opinion, to suppose
that the only Christian witness is the explicit witness
that constitutes the Christian religion. It is characteristic of any religion, including Christianity, that it
neither is nor can be the only witness to the faith of
which it is the most explicit primary expression. The
reason for this is that the same faith that is *explicitly*
expressed through the specific cultural forms of
religion is and must be *implicitly* expressed through
all the other cultural forms — morality and politics,
technology and the arts, and so on. Because this is
so, there is not only the *explicit* Christian witness that
is properly borne through specifically religious words
and deeds but also the *implicit* Christian witness that
can and should be borne through every nonreligious
word and deed as well.

In this connection, I always recall a statement of
Alexander Miller that "to give men bread is not to
affirm that they live by bread alone, but to witness
that we do not."[5] I submit that the witness in such a
case goes even further, attesting to other persons that,
in the final analysis, they do not live by bread alone,
either. In this way, not only our explicit Christian witness to Jesus as the Christ but also whatever we say
or do to meet even the most ordinary human need
always witnesses to the love of God as the gift and
demand of just that existence *in* freedom which is
also existence *for* the freedom of others.

I will not venture to judge to what extent Luther
might have concurred in this insistence that there is
an implicit as well as an explicit Christian witness.
When he speaks of bearing witness as "the first and

5. Alexander Miller, *The Renewal of Man: A Twentieth
Century Essay on Justification by Faith* (Garden City, N.Y.:
Doubleday & Co., 1955), p. 126.

highest work of love that a Christian ought to do," his implication, clearly, is that there are also other works of love, even if they are all secondary to and lower than the one preeminent work of bringing others to faith. Obviously, one way of understanding this implication would be to suppose that Luther assumes something like the same distinction I have made here in order to represent bearing explicit witness to Christ as the first and highest work of a Christian, relative to the implicit witness constituted by all the other works of love. But my guess is that this would be to overinterpret Luther's meaning, reading into his statement a distinction he hardly assumes. In any case, I should myself prefer to see a somewhat different point in the statement, whether or not Luther himself ever intended to make it.

As it happens, it is the same kind of point that Luther himself makes elsewhere in his interpretation of the Ten Commandments, when he takes the First Commandment to be first in another and deeper sense than simply being first in an ordinal series. Rightly understood, he argues, the First Commandment is the *only* commandment, since it calls for that whole and undivided trust in God and loyalty to God that comprise all of human obedience. Thus Luther insists that it is precisely faith that is the fulfillment of the First Commandment, even as sin is its transgression, and he interprets the other nine commandments as all entirely dependent for their force on it, being in effect, specific ways of expressing the one demand that we trust solely in God and be faithful to no one else.[6] My conviction is that it is in the very

6. Theodore G. Tappert (ed.), *The Book of Concord: The Confessions of the Evangelical Lutheran Church* (Philadelphia: Muhlenberg Press, 1959), pp. 342-344.

same way that we should understand what Luther
means when he speaks of the "first and highest work
of love that a Christian ought to do." The bearing
witness to God's grace to which he undoubtedly refers
is not merely one work of love alongside all the
others, even if the first and highest. Rather, its being
the first and highest means that it is rightly understood as the *only* work of love, the one work to which
the other works are all supposed to contribute, being,
in effect, specific ways of bearing witness to God's
strictly universal work of love. Thus, as important as
it is to insist on the implicit as well as the explicit
form of Christian witness, it is even more important
to recognize that the witness to God's love of which
both are forms is not merely one work of love among
others but comprises all the works of love that a Christian ought to do.

This means that the whole of Christian existence
may be said to be an existence for freedom. If all the
works of love are comprised in bearing witness to the
love of God, and if the whole point of such witness
is to attest to the ground of others' freedom as well
as our own, then "existence for freedom" applies to
all that Christians say and do, not merely to some of
it. Of course, Luther's own way of putting the matter reminds us that all that a Christian ought to do
is covered by the phrase, "the works of love." To exist
in faith is not only to trust in God's faithfulness to us
but also to be faithful to God, and this means to be
faithful as well to all those to whom God is faithful.
But to be faithful to God and to all to whom God is
faithful is precisely what it means to love them, just
as God's love for us is nothing other than God's faithfulness to us. So we can understand exactly what Paul
means when he speaks of "faith working through
love." Unless I am mistaken, however, the one test of

whether love is really present is always freedom —
both in the sense that the test of whether one loves
another is always whether one intends to speak and
act in such a way as somehow to optimize the limits
of the other's freedom, and in the sense that the test
of whether one is loved by another is always whether
the limits of one's own freedom are in some respect
thus optimized by what the other says and does.

But if the test of love's real presence in both of
these senses is always freedom, there can be no doubt
whatever that faith is existence for freedom as well
as in freedom. For if anything is certain about faith,
to judge from Scripture and its apostolic norm, it is
that to exist in faith is to exist in love: love of God
and, in God, of all those whom God always already
loves.

The conclusion of this chapter, then, is that faith
in God is indeed the existence of freedom in the
twofold sense that it is both existence in freedom and
existence for freedom. Because faith is utter trust in
God's love as well as utter loyalty to God and God's
cause, it is both the negative freedom *from* all things
and the positive freedom *for* all things — to love and
to serve them by so speaking and acting as to respond
to all their creaturely needs. In this respect faith is
existence *in* freedom, and so a *liberated* existence —
an existence liberated by God's redeeming love. But
because faith is utter loyalty to God and God's cause
as well as utter trust in God, it is also existence *for*
freedom, and so also a *liberating* existence — an existence devoted to so bearing witness to God's love by
all that we say and do as to optimize the limits of
others' freedom in whatever ways this can be done.

The discussion will have already indicated that
there are, in fact, two basic ways in which what we
can say or do can optimize the limits of others'

freedom by bearing witness to them of God's love. There is, first of all, the way of bearing explicit witness to the redeeming love of God re-presented in Jesus Christ, which is the only ultimate ground of all others' liberation as surely as it is of our own. Then, secondly, there is the way of bearing implicit witness to God's love which consists in saying and doing all the countless other things that answer to creaturely needs, and hence also optimize the limits of freedom. In the next chapter, I shall argue that these two basic ways in which our words and deeds can optimize the limits of freedom are, in fact, our ways of participating in God's own liberating work. But all that I need underscore here is that the liberating existence, or existence for freedom, that is of the essence of faith in God is itself not simple but complex — or, rather, duplex — being, as we shall see, a participation in both the redemption and the emancipation that together constitute the liberating work of God.

CHAPTER 3

God as the Ground of Freedom: The Redeemer and the Emancipator

Our task in these chapters is to contribute toward a more adequate theology of liberation than has as yet been achieved and to do so by working out the understanding fundamental to any such theology. This means that our central concern is so to clarify the essential meaning of Christian faith in God that it can be understood to be the answer to the question of freedom. Thus we have recognized that the primary terms of our discussion are "faith" and "freedom," and in the preceding chapter it became clear that the second term may indeed be used to interpret the meaning of the first — to the point, in fact, of allowing us to say that existence in faith *is* the existence of freedom, in the twofold sense of existence *in* freedom and existence *for* freedom.

But it will also have become clear that if the meaning of "faith" may thus be understood in terms of "freedom," this is only insofar as the meaning of "freedom" may itself be interpreted in terms of "faith" — with the result that if faith in God may be said to be the existence of freedom, one may also say that the only authentic existence of freedom is faith in God. In this way, the question of men and women today

concerning the nature and ground of human freedom is answered by transforming it in terms of Christian faith's own essential witness to the God whose
service is perfect freedom.

This explains why, having explicated the meaning of God for us, we must now proceed to explicate
the being of God in itself. If the only authentic existence of freedom is faith in God, the question concerning the nature of freedom is inseparable from
the question concerning its ground, and it is only
when this second question has also been answered
that the answer already given to the first will itself
be fully explicit. Of course, the starting point for this
second explication is one and the same with that for
the first — namely, the Christian witness of faith to
Jesus as the Christ, understood by reference to its
apostolic norm. Just as this witness is the re-presentation to everyone whom it encounters of the possibility of faith in God's love as the gift and demand
of radical freedom — of existence *in* freedom and *for*
freedom — so it is also, at one and the same time, the
assertion that the mysterious whole encompassing
our existence is the God whom Jesus represents as
Father, and so nothing other than pure unbounded
love. Consequently, even as the explication of existence in faith in the preceding chapter could not be
carried out except by constantly referring to its
ground in God's own being and action, so the explication that must be undertaken here of the being and
action of God cannot be achieved except by constantly referring to our own possibility of existing and acting in faith. Even so, there is an important difference
of emphasis between the one task and the other, and
it is only after both have been carried out that we
will have achieved the fundamental understanding
that any theology of liberation must share.

This needs to be emphasized all the more strongly, since, as I argued in chapter 1, this is one of the points where the already existing theologies of liberation have been notably unsuccessful. Presumably because they are so intensely preoccupied with the admittedly urgent issues of action and justice, as distinct from questions of belief and truth, they tend to be far more successful in explicating the meaning of God for us — for our own liberating praxis, as they typically say — than in explicating the being of God in itself. As a matter of fact, aside from certain notable exceptions among the Roman Catholic liberation theologians working in Latin America — I am thinking especially of Juan Luis Segundo — the liberation theologies are characteristically lacking in anything that could be called a "theology" in the strict and proper sense of an adequately developed doctrine of God. Typically, they ignore altogether the questions of fundamental theology concerning the concept and existence of God, and even the more properly systematic theological questions of the being and action of God they tend to deal with only incidentally in the course of explicating the meaning of God for us as the gift and demand of freedom. Not surprisingly, therefore, the existing theologies of liberation typically show signs of still being very much under the influence of a metaphysical understanding of God that has played a fateful role in Christian theology. Because they fail to do their own metaphysical thinking consistently with what they themselves take to be the existential meaning of faith in God, they tend simply to perpetuate uncritically the well-known concept of God of classical metaphysics.

I say there is nothing surprising about this because the only alternative to a good metaphysics, when one undertakes to explicate the beliefs about

God implicit in the Christian witness, is a bad metaphysics; and one of the ways of virtually insuring that
one's metaphysics will be bad is to take it over incidentally and uncritically instead of deliberately and
reflectively. In fact, not even a deliberate and reflective approach to the metaphysical question of the
being and action of God in itself is sufficient if one
allows one's consideration to be confined to too restricted a range of metaphysical alternatives. This becomes almost poignantly apparent in the case of as
good a book as Segundo's *Our Idea of God*.[1] Even
though, unlike most liberation theologians, Segundo
is very definitely concerned to work out a metaphysical understanding of God and, moreover, is well
aware that classical metaphysical theism simply will
not do, his acquaintance with the real alternatives for
doing this and with all the resources that are actually available is so limited that his project is doomed
to fail from the outset. Naturally, no one can be held
accountable for not knowing more than one is able
to know. But anyone who does know more, or, at any
rate, thinks one does, certainly is accountable for ex-
tending the range of alternatives for reasoned choice
and for employing such other resources as are, in
fact, available.

Here I must simply confess that I think those of
us who are acquainted with certain other contemporary expressions of a genuinely postliberal theology can very well be held accountable for doing exactly this. This seems to me particularly true of any
of us who are familiar with so-called process theology, as well as the "process philosophy" lying behind

1.   Juan Luis Segundo, S. J., *Our Idea of God,* trans. John
Drury (Maryknoll, N.Y.: Orbis Books, 1974).

it. In fact, I am confident that it is precisely the metaphysics that has been worked out by certain of the process philosophers — notably, Alfred North Whitehead and Charles Hartshorne — that goes beyond all the usual metaphysical alternatives and provides the very resources that are required if the project of a theology of liberation is to be carried out to completion. The reason I can speak with such confidence is that one of the ways — and, in my opinion, the most adequate way — of describing what process metaphysics is all about is to say that it is the metaphysics that takes "freedom" as its key concept.

I should explain that, as I am using the term here, "metaphysics" refers to that form of critical reflection which seeks to make fully explicit and understandable the most fundamental presuppositions of all our experience and thought, or, as I may also say, the most universal principles that are the strictly necessary conditions of the possibility of anything whatever. Because these presuppositions or principles are radically more fundamental or universal than any other, they can be understood in terms of our ordinary concepts only by analogy, or by generalizing these concepts well beyond the limits of their ordinary uses. Thus one metaphysics differs from another primarily because of the concepts, especially the key concept, it chooses to generalize and because of the consistency or thoroughness of its generalizations. What I should say about process metaphysics, then, is that it differs from every other because of the consistent and thoroughgoing way in which it generalizes the key concept of "freedom."

Of course, one might well suppose from the title usually given to it that it is "process" rather than "freedom" that must be the key concept of process metaphysics. But the reply to such a supposition is that what the process philosophers I have in mind mean when they use the concept "process" is simply the process of creative synthesis, or self-creation, whereby whatever becomes actual does so only by freely synthesizing into a new unity the multiplicity of data provided by the free self-creations of others. In other words, for process metaphysics, to be anything actual at all is to be a free response to other freedom — or, more exactly, to the results of other freedom in the form of the many other things themselves already actual. Because this is so, one may go so far as to say that process metaphysics is precisely *the* metaphysics of freedom, which insists on the applicability of its key concept to literally everything that can be actual at all, from the least particle of so-called physical matter to the God than whom, in Anselm's words, "none greater can be conceived."

The Concept of God in Process Metaphysics

So that it will become even clearer why process metaphysics is just the metaphysics that an adequate theology of liberation requires, I want to characterize briefly how it generalizes the concept of freedom and thereby achieves a distinctive understanding of ultimate reality, and hence of the strictly ultimate reality of God. I will also try to show that the significance of this general understanding of things for Christian theology is directly due to its differing at two absolutely critical points from the traditional metaphysics presupposed by classical Christian theism.

The characteristic claim of process metaphysics, I have said, is that to be anything actual at all, whether the least such thing that can be conceived or the greatest, is to be an instance of process, or creative synthesis, and, therefore, a free response to the free decisions of others already made. This means that anything actual both freely creates itself by responding to the self-created others already actualized and belonging to its past and then contributes itself, along with these others, to the still other self-creations as yet unactualized and belonging to its future. But if this be the metaphysical nature of things, and thus of anything that is so much as coherently conceivable, two consequences follow that are of critical theological importance.

In the first place, it follows that *nothing whatever, not even God, can wholly determine the being of something else*. Taken in a completely generalized, analogical sense, "freedom" means self-creation and, therefore, determination by self in contrast to determination by others. Assuming, then, as process metaphysics maintains, that freedom in this sense is a strictly universal metaphysical principle, one must infer that anything that is even conceivably actual is and must be, in its own way or to its own degree, self-created. This need not mean and, as we shall see, must not mean that self-creation ever occurs in the complete absence of creation by others, any more than creation by others ever occurs in the complete absence of creation by self. But since it clearly belongs to the very idea of freedom as self-creation to exclude being completely determined by others, what anything is, is always, in part, the result of its own free decision, as distinct from the decisions of others that it must somehow take into account.

This implies that even the greatest conceivable power over others — the "omnipotent" power than which none greater can be conceived — could not be all the power there is. Because everything that is anything at all must in part determine itself, it to this extent has a power of its own, distinct from every other, even the greatest conceivable. Consequently, all that could be coherently meant by "omnipotence" is all the power that any one thing could be conceived to have, consistently with there being other things having lesser powers over which it alone could be exercised. Supposing, then, that the thing having such omnipotent power were also "omnibeneficent," in the sense of being good for others to an extent than which no greater can be conceived, one would have the essential theistic concept of God as the one thing or individual whose power over others and goodness toward them are not even conceivably surpassable. But even then one would be forced to conclude that the only possible aim of a God so conceived would not be wholly to determine the decisions of others — since that, not being coherently conceivable, is impossible — but rather, by means of God's own free decisions, to optimize the limits of all of theirs. By this I mean that the God whom a process metaphysics allows one to conceive would so act as to set limits to the freedom of others such that, were the limits other than they are, the ratio of opportunity for good to risk of evil would be unfavorable. Thus, if God allowed others either more or less freedom than they actually have, there would be more chances of evil than of good resulting from their decisions, rather than the other way around.

There will be little question in any informed mind that the understanding of God in relation to others that is thus indicated is strikingly different from that of the classical Christian theism which is still widely supposed to be the only metaphysical theism there is. Given the very different metaphysics that such classical theism presupposes, God alone is thought to be self-creative, everything else being wholly created by God. Thus, according to the classical understanding, God is said to be able to do everything that is not logically self-contradictory, and so God's omnipotence is held, in effect, to be all the power there is. Consequently, supposing God also to be omnibeneficent, one has to allow that God can be held accountable for so determining the course of events that there is only good and nothing evil. This explains, of course, why classical Christian theism staggers under the burden of an admittedly insoluable problem of evil. Because its concept of God's omnipotence necessarily implies that God alone is really free and creative, it cannot both admit the reality of evil and still maintain that God is all-good as well as all-powerful, except by the desperate expedient of dignifying what gives every appearance of being a contradiction with the very different connotations of the word "mystery."

To be sure, many classical theologians, past and present, have thought to solve the problem of evil by insisting that man and woman, at least — along, possibly, with such other rational creatures as angels — are genuinely free and self-creative and, therefore, may be charged with responsibility for such evil as undoubtedly exists. Aside from the fact that so-called natural, as distinct from moral, evil is hardly accounted for by such a "free-will defense," there is the serious question of how there can even be such a thing as creaturely freedom, given the insistence of classical theism that God alone is self-creative, and hence possesses all the power there is. In short, even if one grants, as I certainly would, that classical theologians often talk of human freedom, and even of the role of "secondary causes" generally, there remains ample room to doubt whether they can talk in this way consistently, given what they themselves otherwise assert or imply to be the case.

But, as I have said, there is a second important theological consequence of taking "freedom" to be the key concept of metaphysics. It also follows that *whatever is, even God, is in part determined by the being of other things*. Because anything actual is a creative synthesis of data already given, nothing actual can be the result solely of its own decisions, as distinct from the decisions of others. On the contrary, to be actual at all is to be really, internally related to other things, in the sense that what they are, being synthesized into one's own actuality, thereby partly determines it. But if this is true of all things, just insofar as they are actual, then no actual thing whatever, not even the unsurpassable thing or individual God, can be supposed to fit the classical metaphysical definition of a substance as — in Descartes' formulation — "that which requires nothing but itself in order to exist." As a matter of fact, it is God, least of all, who can be supposed to fit this definition. For if God cannot be conceived except as the all-perfect or unsurpassable one, the one than whom none greater can be conceived, then the only way coherently to conceive God, assuming that everything actual must be related to other things, is as related to *all* things — as the one individual to whom literally everything makes a difference because it in part determines God's own actual being.

That such a universal relativity to all things is indeed a unique property that could not conceivably belong to anyone but God seems clear enough. Just as our own power over others is limited, being power over only *some* others, so it is that only *some* other things have any power over us, in the sense of making any real difference to us by in part determining our

actual being. In fact, prior to our birth nothing whatever made any difference to us, and after our death
nothing whatever will make any such difference, unless we assume that, in some way or other, we survive
our apparent mortality and continue to exist as ex-
periencing subjects. What is more, even of all the
things that happen during our lifetime, we are effectively touched by hardly any. But it seems just as clear,
if you think about it, that a unique individual so radically unlike us as to be effectively touched by literally everything could neither begin nor end (lest it not
be touched, after all, by the things occurring either
before its beginning or after its end), and, therefore,
would be in principle indistinguishable from the unique individual who also effectively touches everything, in that it in part determines the being of all
other things by optimizing the limits of their own free
decisions. In short, the God whose own actual being
literally everything else in part determines is the
same God whose existence as such is determined by
nothing else, because, as the one unsurpassable individual, God's is the one actual being by which
literally everything else is also in part determined.

And yet, once again, no one who is well informed
would wish to deny that a God so conceived is strikingly different from the God conceived by classical
Christian theism. According to the exponents of such
theism, present as well as past, God is to be identified
metaphysically as the Absolute, which cannot be really or internally related to anything and to which,
therefore, literally nothing can make any difference,
because it cannot even in part determine the
Absolute's actual being. Of course, classical theists,
whose metaphysical assumptions require that they
conceive God in this way, have nevertheless continued
to speak, as religious persons ordinarily do, of God's

knowing and loving the world, even as they have continued to say that the whole purpose of man and
woman, as well as of the creation generally, is to serve
God and live their lives to God's glory. But here, too,
there is a serious question of consistency — in this
case, whether such religious talk, implying, as it all
does, that things really do make a difference to God,
can even begin to be made consistent with the underlying metaphysical assumptions, which deny that God
can be really related to anything whatever and that
anything at all can make any difference to God.
Moreover, the familiar classical doctrine that such ordinary talk about God has at least a "symbolic" or
"analogical" truth is hardly reassuring. For the
suspicion remains that the reason God cannot be
literally said to know or love the world is that God
can be literally said not to do so.

This discussion of the theological consequences
of process metaphysics, over against the traditional
metaphysics by which so much Christian theology has
been shaped, ought to give some idea of why I regard
process metaphysics as an indispensable resource for
developing an adequate theology of liberation. This
discussion should also serve to clarify the essential
concepts of the doctrine of God as the ground of
freedom, as both the Redeemer and the Emancipator,
that I must now try briefly to sketch.

God as the Redeemer and the Emancipator

We learned in chapter 2 that the faith which is
the existence of freedom is rightly understood as itself the effect of God's grace, in that it is the prevenient action of God's love that is the necessary condition of the possibility of such faith. It should also

be clear from what has already been said that the proper theological name for God's love, so far as it is the ground of the possibility of faith, is "redeeming" or "redemptive." God, considered in the same respect, is properly said to be "the Redeemer."

The question now is what it is about the very being of God in itself that is properly meant when one speaks in this way. My answer is that theological talk about God as the Redeemer, and hence about God's love as redeeming, or the process of redemption, is rightly understood metaphysically when it is taken to refer to the ever-new event of God's own self-creation in response to the free self-creations of all creatures. In other words, I understand redemption to be the unique process of God's self-actualization, whereby God creatively synthesizes all other things into God's own actual being as God.

If one accepts this answer concerning what we mean metaphysically by "redemption," or by "God the Redeemer," there is evidently a sound basis for speaking, at least symbolically or analogically, of the all-embracing love of God. As we ordinarily use the term "love," to love another person is to do something that always has two closely related aspects. First of all, it is to accept the other person, in the sense of taking him or her into account, allowing him or her to make a difference by partly determining one's own actual being. Then, secondly, it is to act toward the other person, in whatever one says or does, on the basis of such acceptance. Accordingly, as different as God's love would certainly have to be from our own, or any other merely creaturely love, it could nevertheless be conceived to be like them in having these same essential aspects: first, the acceptance of others — in God's case, the acceptance of *all* others — and then, secondly, action directed toward others — *all* others — on the basis of such acceptance.

But, clearly, for God thus to accept all creatures in the sense of creatively synthesizing all of them into God's own everlasting life, is for God to redeem all creatures, in that God thereby delivers them from the meaninglessness of not making any difference to anything or anyone more enduring than themselves. This presupposes, naturally, that the defining characteristic of all creaturely existence is its radical contingency — its being such that, although it exists, it need not exist, and might not exist at all. The evidence for this is that there once was when it was not, even as there will be when it will not be any more. Because it is just such contingency that defines our creaturely existence, the difference that we as creatures can make to one another is always limited by the same radical contingency, which keeps any of us from making more than an extremely limited and short-term difference to those who come after us. If the only contribution our lives could make were the contribution they make to other creaturely lives as limited as our own, they would make no abiding difference and, in that sense, would be meaningless. Death and transience — the perpetual perishing of all things in the ever-rolling stream of time — would be the last word about each of us, and about all of us together.

But if the difference we make is not only such difference as we can make to our fellow creatures but also, and definitively, the difference we each make to God, the one to whom *all* things make a difference and to whose life each thing can contribute *all* that it is, then our lives and all lives are redeemed from meaninglessness by being given an imperishable meaning in the everlasting life of God. In this sense,

all things exist, finally, not merely for themselves or
for one another, but, as the Christian witness has clas-
sically affirmed, for the glory of God, as contributions
to God's unique and all-encompassing life.

And yet also essential to the historic Christian witness is the promise of redemption from sin, and hence
the assertion that God is the Redeemer from sin as
well as from death and transience. What does this
mean?

The essential point is that any talk of sin presupposes the distinctive capacity that makes us human,
and that would make any other creature that had it
a rational creature like ourselves. I refer to our capacity to be aware in a distinctive way of our own existence and, therewith, of everything else. We not only
exist as every other creature does, but we also know
that we exist, together with others, in an existing
world encompassed by the mysterious whole whence
we all come and whither we all go. This means that
to exist in the distinctively human way is always to
exist in this knowledge of our own existence, and
hence to confront the fundamental option of either
accepting ourselves as the creatures we know ourselves to be, or else rejecting ourselves as creatures by
trying to deny the fact of our creaturehood. What is
properly meant by "sin," in the sense of the word
agreeable to the witness of Scripture and the apostles,
is not moral transgression, however true it is that such
transgression is the inevitable consequence of sin.
Rather, sin is just this rejection of ourselves as the
creatures we know ourselves to be, the root of which
always lies in our having rejected the gift and the
demand of the Creator that never cease to encounter
us in our awareness of ourselves. In this way, sin at
its root is our rejection of God's acceptance of our

lives and of all lives, even as faith is our acceptance
of God's acceptance.

Because God's acceptance is boundless, because it
is the acceptance of all things into God's life, it is an
acceptance even of sinners, even of those who have
rejected God's acceptance in rejecting themselves as
the creatures they inevitably are. In this sense the
love of God, as God's ever-renewed act of taking all
things into God's own everlasting life, is the redemption of God's human creatures not only from death
and transience, but also from sin.

But *redemption* from sin is one thing, *salvation* from
sin, something else. What is properly meant by "salvation" is the process that includes not only the redeeming action of God but also the faithful response to
this action on the part of the individual sinner. As
Augustine put it, "he that made us without ourselves,
will not save us without ourselves." We are saved *by*
grace — by God's redeeming acceptance of our lives
into God's own, notwithstanding the fact of our sin;
but we are saved *through* faith — through our own
trusting acceptance of God's acceptance, whereby
God's redemption of our lives becomes our salvation.

This should suffice to make clear why in speaking of God as the Redeemer we are speaking of the
ground of our freedom from the bondage of sin, as
well as from the bondage of death and transience.
But, as we have seen, to exist *in* such freedom is also
to exist *for* it, in the case of all the others whose need
of redemption is as great as our own. And this means
so to exist and to act that, in whatever we say or do,
we bear witness to them of the redeeming love of
God, which is the ground of their freedom from the
bondage of sin, as well as from the bondage of transience and death. By thus bearing witness to God as
the Redeemer, we ourselves participate in God's

redeeming work in the only way in which we could possibly participate in it. For redemption as such is God's work alone, our own part therein being but to bear witness to this fact, so that all men and women everywhere may not only be redeemed from death, transience, and sin but also saved from them, in the sense of being freed from the bondage of sin for the freedom of faith.

God's being the ground of freedom, however, is not exhausted by God's being the Redeemer, and what we now have to consider is the meaning of the claim that God is also the Emancipator. Here, too, the essential point has already been more or less clearly indicated by my discussion of process metaphysics and, specifically, of its concept of God. It belongs to this concept that God is to be conceived not only as the one to whom all things make a difference — or, in theological terms, as the Redeemer — but also as the one who makes a difference to all things, the one whose own self-creation in response to all creatures in part determines each of their self-creations by optimizing the limits of their free decisions. There are the best of reasons for speaking of God as thus partly determining the being of all creatures simply as the Creator. Given a metaphysics that is at all coherent, the only thing that can be meant, in general, by creating the being of others is so creating oneself as to be part-determinative of the others' own processes of self-creation. Because everything actual is and must be, in part, self-creative, nothing is or can be creator of another in the sense of wholly determining what another is to be — even as nothing is or can be a creature in the sense of having its being wholly determined by another. This means, then, that *the* Creator, the one whose creative power over others is such that no greater creative power can be conceived, can only be the unique individual whose self-creation is part-determinative of the self-creation of *all* others. There is no question, so far as I am concerned, that it is in just this sense that God is, indeed, the Creator and that God's creative action in partly determining the being of all other things is simply the other essential aspect of the same all-encompassing love that, in allowing all things to be part-determinative of it, is also uniquely redemptive.

But while I do not have the least hesitation in saying that God is the ground of freedom because God is the Creator as well as the Redeemer, it seems to me illumining to speak of the creative work of God's love as an emancipating, or emancipative, work and of God, correspondingly, as the Emancipator. Because the creative work of God is but the other essential aspect of the same unsurpassable love of all others that is also redemptive, God's creative power over others is omnibeneficent, or all-good, even as it is omnipotent, or all-powerful. Consequently, God's only aim or intention in exercising power is the fullest possible self-creation of all creatures, and so God unfailingly exercises it to optimize the limits of their own free decisions by establishing such fundamental limits of natural order as allow for a greater possibility of good than of evil to be realized through their exercise of freedom. For this reason, God's creative work is, by its very nature, an emancipative work in that it establishes the optimal limits of all creatures' freedom and thus sets them free to create themselves and one another.

God's creative or emancipative work is so far from being neutral or indifferent that it "take sides," in the sense that God always acts so as to maximize the opportunities for good, while minimizing the risks of evil. Consequently, even though God's acceptance of others is boundless, it in no way implies God's approval of everything, and God's approval of things is, in fact, strictly bounded by the unsurpassable goodness of God's aim.

Thus to say that God is the ground of freedom because God is the Emancipator as well as the Redeemer is to speak of the creative, and hence the emancipative, aspect of God's love, whereby God intends the fullest possible self-realization of each and every creature and infallibly acts to do all that can be done to this end — save only what the creatures themselves have to do, both for themselves and for one another. And this, of course, is why there is a very important difference between the way in which we can participate in God's redemptive work and the way in which we can participate in God's emancipative work. Whereas redemption as such, as distinct from salvation, is God's work alone, in which we are able to participate only by bearing witness to it, emancipation is the work of God in which God is dependent on the co-operation of God's creatures if the intention lying behind it is to be fully realized.

Needless to say, God has an unsurpassable role in this emancipative work, and in this God is not in the least dependent upon anyone. To this extent the other half of Augustine's statement is also true, that the God who will not save us without ourselves nevertheless makes us without ourselves. God makes us without ourselves, namely, because the fact that there is some world for us and our fellow creatures to exist and to act in is no more our own doing than is the fact that there is always a certain relatively fixed and stable order to the world which allows for the possibility of more good than evil being realized through exercising our creaturely freedom. All this is solely God's work, in no way anything that either we or any other creature could even possibly do. But since not even God can wholly determine the being of others, each of them being, if actual at all, in part self-determined, the details of the world that exists and the local orders that come to prevail within the larger, cosmic order that God alone establishes are all co-determined by the creatures themselves. To this not inconsiderable extent, we participate in God's emancipating work of optimizing the limits of creaturely freedom only insofar as we do our own irreplaceable part in realizing the aim by which God's unique part in this work is guided. Accordingly, we may say that, even as God will not save us without ourselves, so God will not emancipate us without ourselves — nor will God emancipate others without our participation in the emancipating work of establishing the optimal conditions of their freedom.

This leads to the important question of just how we go about participating in God's emancipating work. If we recall what was said in the preceding chapter, the first thing to say, obviously, is that optimizing the limits of freedom, which is one and the same with bearing witness to God's love, consists in so speaking and acting in relation to others as to respond to all their creaturely needs. But as helpful as this no doubt is as a general answer to the question, it fails to take account of the important fact that creaturely needs are by no means all on the same level. The deeper need of any creature, apart from such need as it may feel for redemption from death and transience and salvation from sin, is the need to exist in a world sufficiently ordered to permit it to realize its own fullest potentialities. Just because this is so, however, it would seem that we participate in God's emancipative work not only, or primarily, by responding to particular creaturely needs arising within the existing world but also, and crucially, by responding to the need of each creature that the existing world itself permit the optimal exercise of its own freedom of self-creation. This, I take it, is the point Gustavo Gutiérrez wants to make:

> The poor person is the by-product of the system in which we live and for which we are responsible. He is the oppressed, the exploited, the proletarian, the one deprived of the fruit of his labor and despoiled of being a person. For that reason, the poverty of the poor person is not a call for a generous act which will alleviate his misery, but rather a demand for building a different social order.[2]

At any rate, I maintain that, even as God's own emancipating work consists in meeting this deeper creaturely need for a world in which one can freely determine one's own destiny in solidarity with one's fellow creatures, so, too, must the crucial part of our participation in God's emancipating work consist in efforts to respond to this same deeper need — the essential difference between God's part in such work and our own being that God establishes the larger, *cosmic* order of nature, while we are responsible for establishing the smaller, *local* orders that we properly speak of as "societies" and "cultures." This is my way of formulating the essential insight both of the earlier social gospel and of the liberation theologies of our own day. For I, too, wish to claim that by far the most important way in which we participate in God's work of emancipation is to labor for fundamental social and cultural change — the kind of structural

2.   Gustavo Gutiérrez, "Faith as Freedom: Solidarity with the Alienated and Confidence in the Future," in *Living with Change, Experience, Faith,* ed. Francis A. Eigo (Villanova, Pa.: Villanova University Press, 1976), p. 25.

or systemic change in the very order of our society and culture that is clearly necessary if each and every person is to be the active subject of his or her history instead of merely its passive object.

Of course, to speak of the necessity of fundamental change is to acknowledge the inequality and injustice of the existing social and cultural order and, therewith, the necessarily conflictive character of our existence in it. But even as God is not neutral or indifferent to creaturely conflict but always sides with what makes for the good of creatures as against all that makes for evil, so we, too, cannot avoid the conflict of human interests or evade the demand always to take sides with the oppressed against all who oppress them. Nor can we ever rule out the eventuality that we can be obedient to this demand only by using force to oppose those who forcibly destroy the conditions of other's freedom — although we will more likely judge rightly in the whole matter of using force if we recall that, for God and, in a radically more limited way, for anyone else who loves, all opposition to others' interests is an opposition to one's own. Just to the extent of one's love for others, one can oppose them only by opposing something in oneself. The essential point, in any case, is that we can participate in the emancipative work of God only by sharing fully in the conflict of human interests and in the struggle to build a more just and equitable social and cultural order.

In conclusion, I would make two related comments. If one approaches the task of a theology of liberation as I have tried to do in these last two chapters, it is essential to recognize the systematic ambiguity of the term "liberation." By this I mean that this term may be quite properly used in different contexts of meaning to refer to two distinct and, in fact, very different things — namely, redemption and emancipation. To identify these in any way, or to fail consistently to distinguish between them, is to confuse the emancipative work of God with God's redemptive work, the Emancipator with the Redeemer. But just as essential is to recognize that it is *one* God who alone is both Redeemer *and* Emancipator and who, therefore, is the one ultimate ground of our freedom and of the freedom of everyone else. Consequently, to separate emancipation and redemption in any way, or to play them off against one another, is to deny that both are the work of one and the same divine love, and that it is always in both, in their distinct but always integrally related ways, that each of us is given and called to share.

CHAPTER 4

Jesus Christ as the Primal Sacrament of Freedom

Up to this point, we have followed the theological procedure indicated by Luther in his statement that "these two belong together, faith and God."[1] Thus we have first considered the existential meaning of God for us as the existence of faith, which I have interpreted as both a liberated existence *in* freedom and a liberating existence *for* freedom; and, then, in the last chapter, we considered the metaphysical being of God in itself as the ground of this existence of freedom, and God, therefore, as both the Redeemer and the Emancipator. In both chapters, however, I made clear not only that their respective explications of faith and of God are mutually implicative — the meaning of God for us and the being of God in itself necessarily implying one another — but also that the norm for judging either explication to be appropriate can only be one and the same apostolic witness. It is this witness, I argued, that still remains, just as it has always been, the real canon of all Christian witness and theology, even though we

1. Tappert (ed.), *The Book of Concord*, p. 365.

today have no alternative but to locate this canon, not in the New Testament writings as such, but in the earliest stratum of witness that we are now able to reconstruct from them.

This apostolic witness is constituted explicitly by the christological assertion "Jesus is the Christ." However, the evidence provided by the New Testament requires us to recognize not only that this assertion was made explicit by means of a wide variety of formulations, of which "Jesus is the Christ" is only one, but also that in the earliest stratum of Christian witness it was apparently a merely implicit assertion that was not explicitly made at all.

As regards this second point, it is generally agreed that the only sources available to us for historical knowledge concerning Jesus and the origins of Christianity are the so-called synoptic Gospels of Matthew, Mark, and Luke. But literary and form criticism of these Gospels has long since established beyond serious question that they themselves, as they have come down to us, are neither our earliest sources nor anything like straightforward historical sources at all, in the modern sense of these words. Rather, they are, in a broad sense, samples of the preaching and teaching — in a word: the witness — of certain segments of the Christian church in the last quarter of the first century after Christ. Moreover, even the sources of which the Gospels are, in turn, the redaction are at best secondary sources for the events they purport to be about, being primary sources solely for the faith and witness of the Christian communities to which we owe them. Significantly, however, in these very earliest sources — roughly speaking, the narrative pericopes in Mark and the sayings source commonly called Q — there is little or no explicit Christology, in the sense of explicit claims about Jesus, his meaning for us, or his being in himself. This, of course, is why students of New Testament Christology have increasingly come to the conclusion that the beginnings of explicit Christology do not lie in Jesus' own witness, or even, possibly, in the witness of the earliest post-Easter community, but, rather, in the developing reflections on this earliest witness on the part of the later church. Thus, while the earliest stratum of witness is definitely witness to Jesus, it is a witness to Jesus in which he himself appears as a witness — not to himself but to the imminent coming of the reign of God, and to its present gift and demand. Even so, implied by this earliest witness — by the fact *that* it was borne, even if not by *what* it asserted — was a definite claim for the decisive significance of Jesus himself. To this extent, the developing Christology of the early church consisted in more and more explicitly formulating, in some terms or other, the christological assertion already implicit in the witness of the earliest church, as well as, presumably, in Jesus' own witness to the coming reign of God (as attested, e.g., by a saying like Lk 12:8 f.; cf. Mk 8:38).[2]

But even taking all this into account, one must still recognize that the apostolic witness that is the canon for all Christian witness and theology is constituted as such, as distinctively Christian witness, only by the assertion, more or less explicit, that Jesus is the Christ. Indeed, it is just because, or insofar as, this assertion is at least implicitly taken to be true that the Christian understanding of faith and of God is the kind of understanding it is. Conversely, because, or insofar as, Christians understand faith and God in

2. See Marxsen, *The New Testament as the Church's Book*, pp. 97-128, espec. 101.

the distinctive way in which they do, they also take
to be true, even if only implicitly, what is explicitly
asserted in the constitutive christological claim that
Jesus is the Christ — whether or not this claim is expressed in these particular concepts and symbols, or
only in some other equivalent formulation.

It lies in the nature of the case, then, that a *Christology* of liberation, for which faith in Jesus Christ is
understood as the answer to the question of freedom,
definitely belongs to any fully explicated *theology* of
liberation; and this is so, even if one feels constrained
to hold, in keeping with what our sources disclose to
have been true of the earliest and, therefore, normative Christian witness, that an explicit Christology
properly follows the explications of faith and God,
instead of preceding them. This should suffice to explain both why what is to be attempted in this chapter belongs to the task we have set for ourselves and
why, nevertheless, it now comes after what has been
attempted in the preceding two, instead of coming
before them.

The Church as the Primary Sacrament of the
   World'sSalvation

This brings us to our central task in this chapter,
which is to sketch at least the outlines of what I have
called a Christology of liberation. It should be kept
in mind that what holds good of a theology of liberation in general must also hold good of a Christology
of liberation in particular, namely, that it must be an
attempt to understand the meaning of the Christian
witness — which is to say, the witness to Jesus as the
Christ — in terms of the question of men and women
today concerning the nature of authentic freedom

and its ultimate ground. This means that here, too
— indeed, here above all — faith and freedom must
be so understood as to interpret one another, freedom
serving to interpret the meaning of faith in Jesus
Christ, even while faith in Jesus Christ serves to interpret the meaning of real human freedom. Thus,
just as we have seen not only that faith in God may
indeed be interpreted in terms of freedom but also
that the only authentic freedom is precisely faith in
God, so we may also claim not only that faith in Christ
is interpretable as the existence of freedom, but also
that the authentic existence of freedom can and must
be interpreted as faith in Christ.

But this claim that the authentic existence of
freedom must be interpreted as faith in Christ directly raises the issue of Christian exclusivism, the claim
that Christians, and only Christians, enjoy the special
calling of God to the unique privilege of salvation. If
we examine this claim closely, we see that it rests on
a certain kind of Christology, namely, the kind according to which the redemptive work of God, and
hence the gift and demand of grace and faith, are not
only *defined by*, but also *confined to*, the unique historical event of Jesus Christ and the unique tradition of
witness of which this event is the authorizing source.
It follows from this Christology that we as Christians
rightly conceive ourselves as the church that is constituted by this tradition of witness only insofar as we
conceive ourselves as the community of the saved, of
those uniquely privileged to experience the call of
salvation and charged with the responsibility of bringing as many other men and women as possible within
the church, so that they, too, may enjoy the salvation
that is given to be enjoyed only there.

There is little question, I think, that it is just this
understanding of the church and, behind it, this un-

derstanding of Jesus Christ that has been the dominant theological understanding throughout most Christian history, at least during the large part of this history which falls between the Constantinian establishment and the Enlightenment, when Christianity enjoyed a virtually unchallenged hegemony over Western culture. Moreover, it is hardly questionable that those of us in the Protestant churches especially have tended to be nurtured almost entirely in this kind of an exclusivistic understanding both of the church and of ourselves as Christians and of the event of Jesus Christ. And yet it certainly is questionable — and, as I am now going to argue, highly questionable — whether this sort of exclusivism can fairly claim the support of Scripture or of its apostolic norm. One reason for doubting that it can is that the dominant theological tendencies in other situations in which Christians have been aware of themselves as only a minority in the world have not been exclusivistic. Both in the ancient church prior to Constantine and in the modern church concurrently with the gradual breakdown of Christendom, theology has tended to be non- or even anti-exclusivistic as compared with such conventional Christian exclusivism.

Thus, for example, Justin Martyr in the second century could claim that Socrates, like others among both the Greeks and the barbarians who lived according to the Logos, was already a Christian. The proof of this to his mind was that the same demonic powers now responsible for the persecution of Christians obedient to the Logos become flesh were the ulterior causes of Socrates' martyrdom.[3] Or, again, the aged

3. Cyril C. Richardson (ed.), *Early Christian Fathers* (Philadelphia: Westminster Press, 1953), pp. 244, 271-272.

Augustine, bent on retracting his earlier errors, had this to say about his treatise, "Of True Religion":

> Again, in the same chapter, I said 'That is the Christian religion in our times, which to know and follow is most sure and certain salvation.' I was speaking of the name, here, and not of the thing so named. For what is now called the Christian religion existed of old and was never absent from the beginning of the human race until Christ came in the flesh. Then true religion which already existed began to be called Christian. After the resurrection and ascension of Christ into heaven, the apostles began to preach him and many believed, and the disciples were first called Christians in Antioch, as it is written. When I said, 'This is the Christian religion in our times,' I did not mean that it had not existed in former times, but that it received that name later.[4]

Finally, we may mention Gregory of Nazianzus' statement in the funeral oration for his father:

> Even before he entered our fold he was one of us. Just as many of our own are not with us because their lives alienate them from the common body of the faithful, in like manner many of those outside are with us, insofar as by their way of life they anticipate the faith and only lack in name what they possess in attitude. My father was one of these, an alien branch, but inclined toward us by his way of living.[5]

So far as examples from the modern period are concerned, perhaps the most striking among Protestant theologians is Frederick Denison Maurice, who,

    4.   John H. S. Burleigh (ed.), *Augustine: Earlier Writings* (Philadelphia: Westminster Press, 1953), pp. 218-219.
    5.   *The Fathers of the Church*, Vol. 22, ed. Roy J. Deferrari et al. (New York: Fathers of the Church, Inc., 1953), p. 123.

encouraged by the very patristic teaching we have just sampled, set himself against conventional exclusivism by insisting that the object of God's redemptive work through Jesus Christ was not the church but the world. Thus he contended that "God has redeemed *mankind*, that He has chosen a family to be witnesses of that redemption, that we who are baptized into that family must claim for ourselves the title of sons of God, must witness to others that they have a claim to it as well as we."[6]

I find it significant, however, that it is in recent Roman Catholic theology that the theological appropriateness of conventional Christian exclusivism has been most thoroughly called into question. Exemplary in this regard is the work of Karl Rahner, especially his carefully elaborated doctrine of "anonymous Christianity," which picks up just the point about Christianity's being the *name* of the true religion that we have seen to be already present in Augustine as well as, by implication, in Gregory of Nazianzus. Thus, speaking of the Second Vatican Council's Dogmatic Constitution on the Church, Rahner says:

> But here in the conciliar text the Church is not the society of those who alone are saved, but the sign of the salvation of those who, as far as its historical and social structure are concerned, do not belong to it. By their profession of faith, their worship and life, the human beings in the Church form as it were the one expression in which the hidden grace promised and offered to the whole world emerges from the abysses of the human soul into the domain

of history and society. What is there expressed may fall on deaf ears and obdurate heart in the individual and may bring judgment instead of salvation. But it is the sign of grace which brings what it expresses, and not only in cases where it is heard in such a way that the hearer himself visibly and historically joins the band of those who announce and testify to this word of God to the world. The Church is the sacrament of the salvation of the world even where the latter is still not and perhaps never will be the Church. It is the tangible, historical manifestation of the grace in which God communicates himself as absolutely present, close and forgiving, of the grace which is at work everywhere, omits no one, offers God to each and gives to every reality in the world a secret purposeful orientation towards the intrinsic glory of God. . . . the Church is not simply the sign of God's mercy for those who explicitly belong to it. It is the mighty proclamation of the grace which has already been given for the world, and of the victory of this grace in the world.[7]

It was, of course, just this kind of non-, indeed, anti-exclusivistic ecclesiology that to some extent helped to shape the ecclesiological reflections of the Second Vatican Council — to the extent, at any rate, that one of the dominant themes in those reflections is that the visible church comprising God's pilgrim people is precisely as such "the sacrament of the salvation of the whole world" (*sacramentum salutis totius mundi*).

Just this theme is given a particularly forceful statement by Juan Luis Segundo, who argues that, if the church is necessary, this is not because its absence would mean the absence of grace from the world, but

7. Karl Rahner, S. J., *The Christian of the Future*, trans. W. J. O'Hara (New York: Herder & Herder, 1967), pp. 82-83.

because without the church the grace always already present in the world would not be *signified*. Thus, so far from being a different road from that travelled by other men and women, which Christians have been called to travel thanks to some privilege granted exclusively to them by God's revelation in Christ, the Christian road is "the same road" travelled by all: "the road of self-giving through love." Christians differ from other human beings only in that, through God's decisive revelation in Christ, "they know the mystery of the journey [on which all are embarked]. And what they know, they know in order to make a contribution to the common quest." Theirs is not "a different road," but "a new responsibility." "The Church is, essentially and primarily, a *sign*." Hence her primary preoccupation "is not directed toward her own inner life but toward people outside. Unlike other organizations founded for the benefit of [their] own members, the Church is a community sent to those who live, act, and work outside her own narrow limits." In sum: the whole purpose of the church is to be a "sign-bearing community."[8]

It will be recalled from earlier chapters that I understand the whole meaning of Christian faith to be an existence in freedom and for freedom, in the sense that, on the basis of trust in the redemptive love of God, the Christian lives in loyalty to God's love, bearing witness to it, by all that he or she says or does, as the ground of all others' freedom even as of his or her own. But, clearly, this is already to say in so many words that to exist as a Christian is to be a sign, an efficacious sign or sacrament, of the all-redeeming

8. Juan Luis Segundo, S.J., *The Community Called Church*, trans. John Drury (Maryknoll, N.Y.: Orbis Books, 1973), pp. 32, 24, 81.

love of God. If we then add the insight that this redemption of which Christians as such are the sign is not confined to, although it certainly is defined by, their witness, then the way is open to a very different understanding of the exclusivism, not only of Christianity and the church, but also of the event of Jesus Christ. According to this alternative understanding of exclusivism, the church which is the sacrament of the whole world's salvation is not the only locus of God's redeeming love, because this love, being strictly universal and all-embracing, is always already effectively presented to every human existence in and through this very existence. Therefore, one must say, not that the church is the only sacrament of God's love, but that the only love that is thus truly redeeming is the love of God of which the church is the sacrament. This, I take it, is the understanding of exclusivism already indicated by Luther's words in "A Mighty Fortress": "And there is no other God."

It remains now to consider briefly the kind of Christology that is necessary to provide the foundation for this true exclusivism of the Christian church and witness.

Jesus Christ as the Decisive Re-presentation of Freedom

I have tried to epitomize the sort of Christology I envisage being required here by the title I have given this chapter; that is, it is a Christology according to which it is precisely Jesus Christ who is the primal sacrament of freedom. The language here is the language of recent Roman Catholic theology, which commonly distinguishes between the church as the *primary* Christian sacrament and Christ him-

self as the *primal* Christian sacrament. I find this a
happy and useful distinction, because the witness of
the church by its very nature points beyond itself to
the event of Jesus Christ as its own origin and principle. Thus it is *this* event, as distinct from the church
of which it is the authorizing source, that is indeed
the primal sacrament — the one efficacious sign of
the redeeming love of God, really present through
this event, to which all Christian faith and witness
are by their very nature the response.

Of course, the primal sacrament of Jesus Christ
is and can be present only in and through the sacrament constituted by the church's witness of faith —
just as, according to the classical Protestant understanding of *solus Christus* and *sola scriptura*, the Christ
who alone is king, and thus king even of Scripture,
is nevertheless none other than the Christ to whom
Scripture alone is the primary witness. To this extent,
there is every reason to speak of the church itself and
as such as the primary sacrament, even as, according
to the New Testament, not only Christ himself but
the apostles also can be said to be the foundation of
the church (cf. Eph 2:20 and Rev 21:14 with 1 Cor
3:11). Just as all Christian faith and witness are and
must be apostolic, so all Christian faith and witness
necessarily depend on the one sacrament which is
constituted by the same apostolic witness, which is to
say, the visible church itself. Even so, all Christian
faith and witness, including apostolic faith and witness, are authorized by a source beyond themselves
in the event of Jesus Christ that is both their origin
and their principle. And because this is so it is the
event of Christ itself that we must speak of as the
primal Christian sacrament and as such the primal
sacrament of the whole world's salvation.

What it means to speak thus of a primal sacrament, however, I have tried to indicate by the subtitle of this second main part of the chapter: to say that Jesus Christ is the primal sacrament of freedom is to say that Jesus Christ is the decisive re-presentation of freedom. But this needs to be unpacked if it is to serve the purpose of a clearer understanding of the event of Christ. This may be done by briefly making five main points:

1. To be a human being is not only to exist as all creatures do but also to understand that one exists and, therewith, to understand the meaning of reality as such and thus, in principle, whatever can be understood: the world of others in real, internal relation with which one alone exists, and the encompassing whole of reality that is the primal source and the final end both of oneself and of the world.

2. But this complex reality of self, others, and the whole, which is presented to our existence in and through the implicit understanding that makes us human, can also be re-presented (i.e., presented *again*, or a *second* time) through the explicit understanding of our existence. The media of such explicit understanding are the concepts and symbols, ability to use which is the external, or behavioral, evidence of our endowment with the distinctively human capacity of understanding. Accordingly, what I mean in general by "re-presentation" is simply the explicit conceptualization and symbolization of the complex reality that we do and must understand at least implicitly as soon and as long as we are human at all.

3. Fundamental to all that we can thus conceptualize and symbolize is the reality of our own existence simply as such, as an existence together with others within the mysterious whole whence we all come and whither we all go. In other words, our en-

dowment with understanding enables us to re-present our own existence with others in the world under the gift and demand of God — "God" being one of the principal ways by which human beings have conceptualized and symbolized the primal source and final end of their own existence as well as of everything else. It is just this "capacity for God," indeed, that underlies the particular cultural form of religion, whether the theistic type of religion for which "God" is the constitutive concept and symbol, or any of the other nontheistic types of religion as well.

4. As the variety of types of religion attests, we human beings are naturally religious only in something like the same way in which we are naturally speakers of languages and thus users of concepts and symbols. Although it is the very nature of being human to speak some particular language, no particular language is itself natural, in the sense that, being human, we all naturally speak it. Similarly, although it is our very nature as human to be religious in some way or other (in the sense of speaking about our existence with others in the world in relation to encompassing mystery, and of asking about the ultimate meaning of our existence, given the identity of this ultimate mystery), there is no particular religion that as such is the natural religion of all human beings. On the contrary, all particular religions are historical rather than natural, in that they are emergents in the course of the historical development of human individuals and communities.

5. The existence of all the particular religions makes the question of *the* religion an urgent human question. Faced as we are not only with the existential question of the ultimate meaning of our existence but also with the various answers to this question re-presented by the several religions — it being

the very nature of a religion to re-present some answer to this question — we are inevitably led to ask for the decisive re-presentation which, were it to be given, would enable us and anyone else to decide truthfully between the conflicting claims and counterclaims of all the particular religions, each of which, by its very nature, claims to be thus decisive.

All this and more, then, is involved in speaking of the event of Jesus Christ as the decisive re-presentation of freedom and, in this sense, as the primal sacrament of freedom. By speaking in this way, I mean that the event of Jesus Christ is the re-presentation of our ultimate possibility in face of the encompassing mystery of our existence as the possibility of freedom — of existence *in* freedom and *for* freedom — and of this mystery itself, correspondingly, as the pure unbounded love that is the only conceivable ground of this freedom. As such, the event of Jesus Christ is the event that permits us to decide truthfully between all the claims and counterclaims of the various candidate revelations, accordingly as they more or less adequately re-present this same gift and demand of radical freedom.

To the central christological question, then, of what is necessarily implied by the constitutive Christian claim that Jesus is the Christ, I answer as follows: what is necessarily implied by this claim is that the event to which its subject term "Jesus" refers is the event in which the gift and demand of radical freedom, which are implicitly presented to our existence in all times and places through our implicit self-understanding simply as human beings, are also made fully explicit in concepts and symbols, and thus decisively re-presented. Moreover, an essential implication of this answer is the insistence that this event, to which the subject term "Jesus" properly

refers, is in principle different from the historical
Jesus, in the sense of a figure out of the past so far
as he is still accessible to us by way of reconstruction
from the synoptic Gospels construed as historical
sources. In my view, just as, I believe, in the view of
all historic Christian witness and theology, from the
apostles right down to the emergence of revisionary
theology in the eighteenth century, the Jesus whom
Christians have affirmed to be the Christ is the Jesus
attested by the apostolic witness of faith, not the so-
called historical Jesus.

Yet just this is another important point where the
theology of liberation toward which I am concerned
to move in these chapters significantly departs from
the theologies of liberation already on the scene. I
argued in chapter 1 that the contemporary liberation
theologies are, in fact, examples of the general type
I characterized as revisionary (including liberal and
postliberal) theology. As open to objection as this argument may have seemed, it is at no point easier to
defend than at the point of the Christology typically
developed by the various theologies of liberation. As
a matter of fact, in what has been widely heralded as
the liberation Christology — namely, Jon Sobrino's
Christology at the Crossroads — one finds a type of christological reflection whose unbroken continuity with
that of the earlier liberal theologies of the nineteenth
century is unmistakable.

This becomes especially clear when one reflects
on what Sobrino takes to be the starting point of his
"historical Christology." Its starting point, he argues,
is the man Jesus insofar as he is accessible to us by
way of historical reconstruction from the Gospels. As
difficult as it may be for us to believe or even to understand it, this position, so widely held today, that
the real norm of Christian witness and theology is

the historical Jesus, is far from being the position of historic Christianity. As we had occasion to observe in chapter 2, the criterion employed by the early church in determining what writings were and were not canonical was in no way the person or message of the historical Jesus. On the contrary, the early church's criterion of canonicity was apostolicity; and the Jesus it understood to be the authorizing source of all Christian existence was none other than the Jesus attested by the apostolic witness which was itself taken to be the primary authority or norm for what is and is not appropriately Christian. As a consequence, the Jesus in whom the overwhelmingly vast majority of Christians have believed from the apostles onward is the Jesus attested by the apostolic witness as the Christ of God, as the decisive re-presentation of the gift and demand of God's own all-embracing love and, consequently, of our own authentic possibility of freedom. Relative to this historic position of the Christian community, the typical notion of revisionary theology in general and of liberation theology in particular, that it is the historical Jesus who is the true Christian canon, is a theological novelty, and, I dare say, one that has long since proved to be seriously misled and misleading. Nothing is more characteristic of the New Testament or of its apostolic norm than that Jesus is represented there not as a human being *with* whom we believe in believing in God (that being, rather, the very role assigned to the apostles), but as the human being *through* whom we believe in believing in God — who is himself the explicit gift and demand of God's grace, and thus of our own authentic possibility of existing in freedom and for it.

Of course, the New Testament takes completely for granted that this Jesus, who is the decisive re-

presentation of God, was a human being; and one
may quite properly infer from this that it understands
Jesus to have believed in God, to have borne witness
to his belief, and so on. Still, the point remains that
it is not this Jesus, this historical Jesus, that the New
Testament writings refer to in witnessing to him as
the Christ. Although they certainly *assume* his
humanity, along with everything that it implies, it is
not his humanity that they are primarily concerned
to *assert*. Rather, their whole point in asserting that
he is the Christ is to place him on the divine, not the
human, side of the relationship between God and
human beings generally. Precisely as a human being
he is understood to be the decisive re-presentation,
and hence the real, sacramental presence, of God to
all humankind.

And this explains, naturally, why there is not a
single writing or tradition in the entire New Testament in which Jesus is understood to be the Christ
of God because of the perfection of his own personal
faith in God. Sobrino's claim that what it means to
say that Jesus is divine is that Jesus is "the first and
foremost of believers," or "the first to have lived as a
resurrected one in history because he fully lived a
life of faith," may well fit what we today find it only
too easy to suppose.[9] But this in no way alters the
fact that such a claim has no basis whatever in the
New Testament. In the entire synoptic tradition,
there is not so much as a single reference to Jesus'
own personal faith, much less any teaching to the effect that the perfection of his faith is the ground of
his being divine. The closest any New Testament writ-

---

9. Jon Sobrino, S. J., *Christology at the Crossroads*, trans.
John Drury (Maryknoll, N.Y.: Orbis Books, 1978), p. 89.

ing comes to talking about Jesus' faith is the Epistle
to the Hebrews, when it speaks of him as "the pioneer
and perfecter of our faith" (12:2). But, significantly,
it is *our* faith, not Jesus', that is spoken of even here;
and it is entirely in keeping with this that Jesus is not
numbered among the cloud of witnesses enumerated
in chapter 11, not even as the first and foremost of
such witnesses. Instead, he is represented there, just
as everywhere else in the New Testament, as the one
to whom all the witnesses properly bear their witness
— as the mediator both of their faith and ours, not
as the subject of a faith of his own. The conclusion is
inescapable that the earliest Christian communities
to which we owe all the traditions concerning Jesus
preserved in the New Testament did not have the
least interest in his own personal faith as a human
being but consistently represented him as the event
that is the origin and principle, and hence the
authorizing source, of their faith and, as they bear
witness, also of ours.

The same must be said of any references in the
New Testament writings to the love of Jesus or to his
obedience, whether the summary references typical
of Paul when he speaks of the love or of the obedience
of Christ (as, e.g., in Phil 2:6ff.; 2 Cor 8:9; Rom 5:18f.,
15:1f.), or the extended, legendary references to
Jesus' obedience to the Father in the temptation
stories set at the beginning of the Gospels or in the
story of his final struggle in Gethsemane, which is
placed just before the account of his passion and
death (e.g., Mt 4:1-11par.; Mk 14:32-42). Without
doubt, all such talk is the talk of believers who already believe in Jesus' decisive significance and are
thereby bearing witness to their faith, and not in any
way trying to set forth certain historical facts on which
their faith is supposedly based. Like the Gospel ac-

counts of Jesus' birth or of his baptism, or of yet other events immediately before and after his crucifixion, all such talk is clearly legendary and has an existential-historical, not an empirical-historical meaning.

But if the New Testament writings do not themselves assert that Jesus is the Christ because he is the one human being whose faith in God was perfect, one may be pardoned for being skeptical whether there is any other way by which such an assertion can be made to claim the support of the New Testament. Certainly, this cannot be convincingly done by the familiar reductive argument from the experienced, or believed, fact that Jesus is the Christ to what would have had to have been the case in order for him to be such. For as valid as such a reductive argument may be in principle, there is not the least reason to suppose that it can be used to justify the claim of Sobrino and others that it is only because Jesus perfectly actualized the possibility of faith in God, thus becoming "the one who first lived a life of faith in all its fullness," that he is properly asserted to be the Christ.[10]

For all these reasons, then, the type of liberation Christology that Sobrino proposes is quite untenable. In fact, I am convinced that the Jesus who is said to be the Christ because he himself is the perfectly true man is simply a projection — a projection of what our own existence of freedom as Christians is mistakenly supposed to require by way of a christological foundation — instead of being in any way the Jesus attested by the apostles and the New Testament to be the decisive re-presentation of our freedom. On the other hand, if we orient ourselves steadfastly to the

10. Ibid.

apostolic witness, and to the consistent witness of the New Testament, as well as of the creeds and dogmas of the ecumenical councils — especially Nicaea and Chalcedon — we can hardly fail to conclude that Jesus is the Christ, not because he *actualized* the possibility of freedom and, unlike us, actualized it perfectly, but because, through the Christian witness of faith, he *re-presents* the possibility of freedom and, for us, re-presents it decisively.

In conclusion, I would observe, in fairness to the theologians of liberation, that they are by no means alone in returning to the inadequate christological project of an earlier liberal theology, instead of moving ahead to the kind of postliberal Christology of liberation that I have outlined here. As a matter of fact, there are few things in contemporary revisionary theology about which there appears to be more consensus than that the foundation of an adequate Christology lies in a historical Jesus who was himself the perfect believer and, for this reason, the Christ of God. If the variation on this common pattern worked out by the theologies of liberation is in any way distinctive, it is solely the consistent and thoroughgoing way in which they interpret the existence of faith as the existence of freedom — as the liberated and liberating existence of which Jesus' own existence is taken to be the perfect actualization. But if I am right, the real promise of a Christology of liberation can never be realized as long as it is allowed to be nothing more than one more variation on this familiar christological pattern, which, having been projected over a century-and-a-half ago by an earlier liberal theology, has already been tried and found wanting. The achievement of an adequate Christology of liberation, such as our situation today both demands and makes possible, waits on the liberation of Christology itself from the excessively narrow constraints within which even the most revisionary christologies continue to be projected. The full story about this form of theological bondage is at least as long as the story about the bondage of theology more generally to the metaphysics of classical Christian theism, to which I alluded in the preceding chapter. But the relevant point here is that an adequate Christology, like an adequate theology generally, depends on just the kind of liberation of theology itself to which this whole book is devoted, but which is the special subject of the concluding chapter.

CHAPTER 5

Subtler Forms of Bondage and Emancipation

If the preceding chapters have succeeded in their purpose, we have now taken some important steps toward a theology of liberation. One such step is to have understood the systematic ambiguity of the concept "liberation," which requires that we distinguish without separating, or that we relate without identifying, the two processes that I have called redemption and emancipation. Both of these processes are quite properly included under the one concept "liberation," because the one as well as the other involves a process of being liberated from bondage. In the case of redemption, it is liberation from the bondage of death, transience, and sin; in the case of emancipation, it is liberation from all the other forms of bondage, particularly the structural or systemic bondage, that keep us and our fellow creatures from realizing our fullest potentialities. But while there is thus a single process of liberation embracing both redemption and emancipation, these two processes are sufficiently distinct from one another that only serious confusion can result from simply identifying them.

This became all the clearer as we took the other important step of explicating the ultimate ground of freedom in the being of God in itself. Although there is indeed one God who is the sole ultimate ground of all freedom, and hence of both processes of liberation, this one God is properly distinguished as both the Emancipator and the Redeemer — God's emancipative and redemptive work being two quite different, even if integrally related, aspects of the one divine reality of all-embracing love. Thus if God as the Redeemer so acts as to accept all things into God's own life, where they alone have an abiding meaning, God as the Emancipator so acts as to optimize the limits of freedom for the self-creations of all of God's creatures.

Grounded as it is, then, in the dipolar nature of God's own being, the distinction between redemption and emancipation is absolutely fundamental to any adequate theology of liberation. Just as fundamental, however, is that both processes are so grounded in the one being of God that neither they nor our own participation in them can ever be separated or played off against one another. The one liberating work of God, in which each of us is given and called to play our part, is a redeeming *and* an emancipating work.

Beyond this fundamental understanding of faith and freedom and of their ultimate ground in the liberating love of God decisively re-presented through Jesus Christ, there is yet a further step I should like to take toward a theology of liberation. I made the statement earlier that the forms of human bondage are necessarily multiple and that there are yet subtler forms than those that ordinarily claim our attention. Among the other things I had in mind in saying this are certain constraints that, as it seems to me, usually keep the whole project of a theology of liberation itself from ever being adequately realized.

One such constraint I drew attention to in chapter 3, when I alluded to the widely held assumption that the only terms in which the being of God in itself can be explicated metaphysically are the terms provided by classical Christian theism. Whether this assumption is made explicitly or only tacitly, making it delimits one's choices either to a metaphysical understanding of God that is profoundly alien to the whole idea of human liberation or else to a theology that settles for thinking and speaking simply of the meaning of God for us, as distinct from the being of God in itself. Consequently, to point to an alternative metaphysical theism, as I sought to do in that same chapter, is, in effect, to emancipate theological reflection from the narrow range of alternatives between which it is supposedly constrained to choose. In a somewhat similar way, the discussion of Christology in the preceding chapter was intended to break out of the constraints by which thinking about Christ is still kept from achieving its object.

But if I am right, there are certain other, still subtler forms of bondage from which theology must also be emancipated if anything like an adequate theology of liberation is to be achieved. Therefore, it is some of these subtler forms of bondage and emancipation that I wish to consider in this concluding chapter — keeping firmly in mind in doing so that here, too, our task is not to develop one theology of liberation among others but rather to move toward such a theology by clarifying what it would necessarily have to share in common with any other that was at all adequate.

Beyond Anthropocentrism

One of the characteristics of situations of inequality is that it is solely by the standards of the haves
that the have-nots tend to measure their disadvan-
tage. Thus, for example, students of American history have pointed out that the political achievement
of Andrew Jackson was to bring a class to power that,
while poorer than the Whig aristocrats of the time,
was just as eager to get rich quickly, and every bit as
committed to economic expansion as the way to do
so. Accordingly, in the battle Jackson waged with the
Bank of the United States for cheap credit as a means
to such expansion, what was resented by those whose
cause he represented was not at all the wealth of the
rich but only their exclusiveness. The common
enemy of Whig and Democrat alike was whoever
stood in the way of economic growth. As it turned
out, that common enemy was the native American.
And so the other side of the much vaunted triumph
of the common man through Jacksonian democracy
was "the trail of tears" of the Cherokee nation. Victor C. Ferkiss, to whom I owe this first example, gives
yet another from American history when he speaks
of the failure at the end of the nineteenth century of
such movements as Henry George's Single Tax movement and Edward Bellamy's Nationalism. Their failure, he argues, was largely due to the fact that

> they, and even the once-promising American
> Socialist party, were not protests against liberal
> society as such, insofar as their supporters were
> concerned, but rather the complaint of those ex-
> cluded from the division of the booty — Jack-
> sonianism in a new guise. As soon as new ships to
> loot hove into view and new towns were found to
> sack these movements faded away, though it took

the repression of the Wilson Administration during
World War I to finally destroy the Socialists as a significant political force. Everyone save a few isolated
intellectuals — men like pioneer ecologist George
Perkins Marsh, naturalist John Muir, or government scientist and explorer John Wesley Powell —
unreservedly embraced liberalism and its doctrine
of the acquisition of wealth through the ruthless exploitation of nature.[1]

This second example, especially, illumines one of
the subtler forms of bondage from which, as I see it,
theology today needs to be emancipated if there is
ever to be anything like an adequate theology of
liberation. I refer to the exaggerated humanism, or
anthropocentrism, for which the larger world of nature is, in effect, the common enemy of the most
varied human groups, advantaged and disadvantaged
alike. If such anthropocentrism, with its presupposed
dualism of history and nature, has been a defining
characteristic of modern Western culture generally,
it has also been typical of the whole movement of
revisionary theology that has sought to come to terms
with modern culture in reflecting critically on the
traditional forms of the Christian witness. It is not
surprising, then, if we recall that it is to just this larger
revisionary theological movement that the various
theologies of liberation also belong, that they, too,
should be marked by the same anthropocentrism.
Whatever the form of bondage to which they may be
oriented — political, economic, cultural, racial, or
sexual — it is solely with *human* liberation that they
are typically concerned, and if they regard non-

1. Victor C. Ferkiss, *The Future of Technological
Civilization* (New York: George Braziller, 1974), p. 42; cf. also
pp. 36-37.

human nature as having any value at all, it is the strictly instrumental value it has for realizing *human* potentialities.

That this is so will seem all the more understandable if we remind ourselves that anthropocentrism in this sense cuts across even extreme differences between alternative understandings of human existence in the contemporary world. Broadly speaking, one may say that, aside from the older understandings mediated by the Christian and other religious traditions, these alternatives include two main types of post-Christian humanism: an older, more evolutionary type, with its ideology of economic growth through science and technology, typical of the highly industrialized societies of the West; and a newer, more revolutionary type, with its ideology of overcoming oppression through the overthrow of the existing order, typical of the other highly developed societies of the East. And yet, as different as these two types of contemporary humanism certainly are, there are many respects in which they are similar, and none is more striking than their respective understandings of the place and value of nonhuman nature.

For the older, more evolutionary type of humanism, from Francis Bacon and John Locke all the way down to the theorists and policymakers of capitalist societies today, nature is understood as having, or, rather, acquiring, value solely through human beings. Lacking in any intrinsic worth of its own, it exists entirely in order to be exploited by human ingenuity and industry in that acquisition of wealth which is the necessary condition of economic growth, and hence of human fulfillment. Nuances aside, however, nature is hardly understood any differently by the other more revolutionary type of humanism, whether by such classical spokesmen as

Karl Marx or by the theorists and politicians of contemporary socialism. Despite Marx's occasional charge that capitalism alienates human beings not only from themselves and one another but also from the nature around them, even he typically assumes that man is the measure of all things and nature an enemy to be conquered. Indeed, Marx understands the conquest of nature through science and technology to be a precondition for realizing the kingdom of freedom. And so socialists today, true to their Marxist heritage, typically share the older liberal goal of unlimited economic growth through science and technology. The gravamen of their complaint against capitalism is simply that its pursuit of private profit tends rather to inhibit than to promote the technological triumph of human beings over nature to which socialism itself is wholeheartedly committed.

There is nothing in the least strange, then, about the anthropocentrism that is so prominent a feature of the theologies of liberation. For from one extreme to the other, this same anthropocentrism characterizes the whole spectrum of the contemporary humanisms with which, in one way or another, each of these theologies is of a piece.

Nor is this all that can be said by way of explaining the typical anthropocentrism of theologies of liberation, as well as of modern Christian theology generally. It is widely agreed that both of the main types of contemporary humanism are properly said to be "post-Christian" in that they both represent a secularization of the understanding of human existence characteristic of Christianity. Consequently, there are those who have argued that it is Christianity itself, or the Judaeo-Christian tradition more generally, that is the original source of the anthropocentrism of modern Western culture. In the form in which this argument has sometimes been stated, it may be easily criticized as simplistic by pointing to a good deal of evidence that tells against it. Since it is precisely the more modern expressions of Christianity that are notably anthropocentric, it is a fair question whether the anthropocentrism of modernity is the effect of Christian anthropocentrism or, rather, its cause.

And yet it would be mistaken, in my judgment, simply to dismiss the argument that traditional Christianity has been important in developing the modern dualism of history and nature and its anthropocentric understanding of human liberation. Not the least reason for saying this is the position taken by certain Christian apologists in the face of criticisms of Christianity that have been made in recent years by a number of persons concerned with our growing ecological crisis. According to these apologists, it is not possible to avoid such criticisms by denying the difference in principle between nature in general and human existence in particular, or by so expanding the concepts of ethics as to allow rights to nature that human beings have the responsibility to respect. On the contrary, by these apologists' own account, biblical religion and theology are sufficiently anthropocentric to require the differentiation of a man or a woman as in an important respect "a non-natural creature" and to preclude assigning enough intrinsic value to anything else in nature to entitle it to be the bearer of even the least right of its own.[2] That at least

2.   Thomas Siger Derr, *Ecology and Human Liberation: A Theological Critique of the Use and Abuse of Our Birthright* (Geneva: WSCF Books, 1973), p. 40. Quotations in subsequent paragraphs expressing the same point of view are all also from this book (pp. 46, 53).

some Christian theologians should find it possible as well as necessary thus to defend an "open, unabashed anthropocentrism" is surely some reason for thinking that theology's bondage to such an anthropocentrism is not merely a function of its alliance with one form or another of modern humanism. Nevertheless, I am convinced that bondage is exactly what it is and that theology today both must and can be freed of it.

Theology *must* be freed from such anthropocentrism because, unless and until it is, it cannot possibly be an adequate theology in either of the respects in which it is called to be so. It cannot be adequate in respect of being credible to human beings today, because, if anything is now worth believing, it is that the dualism of history and nature presupposed by such anthropocentrism is both theoretically false and practically vicious. There is every reason to believe that human existence has emerged from nature and is itself entirely natural. Human existence's most distinctive characteristics, such as the capacity for true speech and self-understanding, realize some of nature's own potentialities, instead of in any way distinguishing it as "non-natural." In fact, so far from indicating that man and woman in any way stand apart from nature and above it, human culture and history are one way — the distinctively human way — of being natural. This means, among other things, that they are subject to the same laws of ecology as apply throughout the ecosphere of nature generally — such laws as that everything is connected with everything else, everything must go somewhere, everything is gained at some cost, and so on. To continue to speak, therefore, as some theologians do, of "nature's hostile territory," and thus to claim that "man is emancipated *from* nature *for* history," is to foster the very attitudes toward our natural environment that have already driven us to the brink of historical catastrophe, whether through the exhaustion of non-renewable resources upon which any progress in history is dependent or through so polluting our natural home that it is no longer humanly habitable.

A theology bound to such anthropocentrism is also inappropriate to the Christian witness of faith itself. Whatever some theologians may say, and however much in the Christian tradition may appear to bear them out, I am persuaded that the most fundamental axioms of biblical faith preclude any such dualism between nature and history. One reason for this is that careful scholars of the creation narratives in Genesis persuasively argue that these narratives are witnesses as much to the essential unity of man and woman with all their fellow creatures as to their unique difference over against them. Thus Claus Westermann points out that "the animals receive the first blessing mentioned in the Bible," and "the same words spoken to the animals, 'be fruitful and multiply,' are used to convey God's blessing to man . . . . This connection between the animals and man . . . is a stronger statement concerning the common relationship between man and the animals than is the assumption of genealogical connections in a theory of evolution."[3]

The crucial reasons for my position, however, in no way depend on the exegesis of particular passages of Scripture, but have to do with the necessary conditions of the possibility of the entire scriptural witness and, in this sense, with what I have referred to

---

3. Claus Westermann, *The Genesis Accounts of Creation*, trans. Norman E. Wagner (Philadelphia: Fortress Press, 1964), pp. 19-20.

as the axioms of biblical faith. Among such axioms, as classical Christian theology rightly recognized, is that not only man and woman but anything whatever is created out of nothing by God, and hence to some degree or other displays the being of its Creator, who is immanent in it as well as transcendent of it. This implies that, while there is an *infinite* difference between God and every creature, there neither is nor could be an *absolute* difference between God and any creature, from which it follows that any difference between creatures themselves, even the unique difference between human creatures and all the others, is and must be a merely *finite* difference. Hence if, according to Scripture, all other creatures are to be loved, finally, solely for the sake of God, then the same is true of human creatures, who are likewise to be loved, finally, solely to God's glory. On the other hand, if God is immanent in human creatures so that, displaying the being of their Creator, they are the bearers of rights that should be respected, then the same is true of all other creatures, each of whom in its own way and to its own degree also displays the being of the Creator, thereby acquiring the intrinsic worth that is the basis of all rights.

Given the scriptural axiom of creation, then, the dominion over the other creatures to which man and woman are uniquely appointed is by no means a matter simply of their stewardship over a nature having merely instrumental value for human history. On the contrary, they are most like the God in whose image they are uniquely created when they so rule over creation as to recognize not only the *difference* in intrinsic value between one kind of creature and another, but also the *unity* in intrinsic value by which all creatures are bound together as the good creation of God.

But if theology must be freed from anthropocentrism to be either appropriate or credible, it also *can* be freed from anthropocentrism because there are conceptual resources available for overcoming all dualism by expressing just this combination of unity and difference between nature and history. That this is so should be evident from my argument in chapter 3 that process metaphysics is the consistent and thoroughgoing generalization of the key concept of "freedom." If, as this metaphysics maintains, to be anything actual at all is to be in part self-creative, and hence an instance of freedom, then even the least actual thing must bear at least some likeness to the eminent freedom of God, who, as the greatest conceivable instance of self-creation, is immanent in all other instances as well as transcendent of them. But this evidently implies, in turn, that anything actual has at least some intrinsic value and that any difference between one kind of actuality and another is at most a finite difference between emergent levels of value corresponding to different emergent levels of freedom. At the same time, a process metaphysics such as this has all the resources necessary for conceptualizing the real uniqueness of human existence. For although there is only a finite difference between human existence and all the other kinds of actual things, human freedom and value are nevertheless emergent properties of a distinctive level of natural existence and as such are irreducible to those of any lower level. In short, just as process metaphysics frees us to talk about the being of God in itself as the ground of freedom, so it also provides the concepts by which we can at last go beyond anthropocentrism in our understanding of human liberation.

The objection that is certain to be made to this argument is that such a nonanthropocentric understanding of liberation is self-defeating. By insisting on the unity of history and nature and the intrinsic value of every creature, it relativizes our proper concern with the liberation of men and women, especially their emancipation from the forms of structural or systemic bondage from which so many of them unjustly suffer. That this, at any rate, is the inherent danger of such an understanding is clear from the fact that much of the recent environmental movement has displayed such an indifference to the demands of social justice that there are grounds for suspecting that it functions as an ideology, as a means employed by the more highly developed societies to discourage the growth of those that are far less so.

My response to this objection is to say, first of all, that I have no intention whatever of playing off a concern for the fulfillment of nature generally against a concern for social justice. To argue, as I have, that every creature on earth has some intrinsic value and, to this extent, deserves to be respected is in no way to imply that all creatures have an equal value or that there are not important differences between the rights of one creature and another. But I find not the least reason to believe, as so many seem to do, that human creatures can be treated as ends in themselves, and hence as more than mere means, only if the rest of earth's creatures cannot. On the contrary, I entirely share the judgment of those who see the closest connections between our treatment of nature generally as mere means and our treatment of our fellow human beings in exactly the same way. From all the evidence known to me, the history of our species' ruthless exploitation of other species is entirely of a piece with the history of our ruthless exploitation of one another. Therefore, I can only agree with Charles Birch when, in replying to much the same kind of objection, he insists that the increasingly negative impact of human beings on the natural environment through ever-expanding growth of population, consumption of resources, and environmental deterioration is directly connected with the persistence of radical inequality between the rich nations and the poor. As he puts it: "There is no chance of the poor countries developing adequately unless the rich countries reduce the huge proportion they contribute to the total impact. This involves a programme of de-development of the rich world. The rich must live more simply that the poor may simply live."[4]

Beyond this, my response to the objection is to say that any theology worthy of the name must be just as concerned with questions of truth as with issues of justice, if only because the only way in which justice in the long run can be achieved is on the basis of truth. If it is correct to argue, as I have, that modern anthropocentrism is true neither to the scriptural axiom of the creation of all things by God nor to the best insights of contemporary science and philosophy, then theology has every reason to go beyond such anthropocentrism even if it also has reason to see that the truth of human solidarity with nature is kept free from ideological misuse. Indeed, any other course would be profoundly unjust to human beings, who have everything to gain from being emancipated from supportive illusions about their own specialness. For it is only so that they may fully assume that dominion over the creation to which they are appointed in being called to rule over their fellow creatures after the image of God's own loving rule — so

4. Charles Birch, "Creation, Technology and Human Survival: Called to Replenish the Eath," *The Ecumenical Review*, 28 (1976): 70.

as not merely to use and to exploit them but also to enjoy and to further them as co-participants in the all-inclusive end of God's reign.

The Emancipation of Theology

Although I have already been speaking about the emancipation of theology from its bondage to anthropocentrism, it will have become clear that, as subtle as this form of bondage may be, it is by no means peculiar to theology, much less to the already existing theologies of liberation. So far as modern Western culture is concerned, at any rate, such anthropocentrism is so pervasive that it has not been until relatively recently, in the face of the mounting ecological crisis, that most of us have even become aware of the extent of our bondage to it. Because this is so, all that I have said about going beyond anthropocentrism, although applied to theology, admits of a much wider application. Indeed, it applies wherever the truth of our human solidarity with other creatures and our responsibility for them is ignored or denied, whether expressly or by implication. But it is quite otherwise with what I take to be an even subtler form of bondage from which theology both must and can be freed if there is ever to be an adequate theology of liberation. In this case, the bondage in question is peculiar to theology, and to speak of emancipation from it, as I now propose to do, is to speak precisely and only of the emancipation of theology.

The form of bondage of which I speak may be indicated by saying that, throughout its history right up to the present time, theology has been understood and done more as a form of rationalization than as a form of critical reflection. This is to assume, of course, the usual, pejorative sense of the term "rationalization," according to which it designates the process of giving reasons for positions already taken as distinct from the process of determining in a reasoned way whether positions already taken are, in fact, worth taking. It will be recalled that, in discussing earlier what is properly meant by "critical reflection," I defined it as the process of determining in a deliberate, methodical, and reasoned way whether something that appears to be the case, or, alternatively, is said to be the case, really is so. But it is precisely not critical reflection in this sense, but, rather, what I have distinguished as rationalization that has almost always been taken to be the proper business of Christian theology. If theology has been conceived to have any properly critical function at all, it has been restricted to criticizing particular witnesses of faith by reference to whatever has been understood to constitute normative Christian witness, whether Scripture and tradition, or, rather, Scripture alone.

To be sure, there has been an important difference between classical Roman Catholic and classical Protestant theology. Whereas the former has been understood to have the task of rationalizing the positions taken by a particular institutional church (namely, the Roman Catholic Church), the latter has been expected to rationalize the positions of that visible church which, being always only more or less visible in the various institutional churches, can never be simply identified with any of them. Notwithstanding this difference, however, in neither case has theology been allowed, much less assigned, the task of critically reflecting on the positions taken by the church in such a way as to ask and answer the radical question as to their truth. On the contrary, theology has been, and, for the most part, still is expected simply to assume the truth of the church's positions and then to occupy itself with giving reasons for them — just this being the sense almost always given to Anselm's famous phrase, taken as describing theology's task: "faith seeking understanding" (*fides quaerens intellectum*).

Of course, this classical understanding of theology has long since been criticized by what I have spoken of as revisionary theology. Insisting that human experience and reason are also criteria of religious and theological truth, revisionary theologians have never been content simply to rationalize positions already taken in the historic Christian witness, but have criticized these positions on the basis of others typically taken by persons sharing in the experience and reflection distinctive of modern Western culture. But even with this revision, the task of theology, significantly, has still been understood less as critical reflection than as rationalization — with the single, if important, difference that the positions to be rationalized by theology have been those of modern secularity as well as those of historic Christianity. Indeed, revisionary theologians have typically understood theology as a rationalization of the Christian witness in terms of secular concerns and questions. If they have also sought to deepen secularity by interpreting it in terms of the Christian witness, they have nevertheless conceived of their efforts as originating in a prior option and commitment to secular self-understanding.

There is no need to repeat here what I said in chapter 1 about the self-criticism of liberal theology effected subsequently by so-called neo-orthodoxy, or about theology's having more recently passed into a genuinely postliberal phase. The pertinent point is simply that, even in these later developments, theology has continued to be understood and done as the rationalization of positions already taken, more than as critical reflection on the worth of such positions. Thus whether the positions in question have been solely those of "the biblical message," as in neo-orthodoxy, or, rather, also those of contemporary secularity, as in much of the postliberal theology of the present time, in either case theology has been conceived as reflection on the basis of such positions instead of reflection directed toward critically establishing their truth.

The even more pertinent point is that the same is true of the concept of theology's task typically expressed or implied by the theologies of liberation. From their standpoint, naturally, all the other ways of understanding and doing theology are more or less seriously inadequate. In fact, they commonly charge that not only classical theology and its liberal revision, but also neo-orthodoxy and the postliberal theology of the present all either are or are in danger of becoming "ideological" in the Marxist sense of the word. The grounds for this charge are that these theologies are all rationalizations of positions already taken either in the historic Christian witness or in modern secularity. As such, they either set forth an abstract understanding of redemption having no positive relation to the concrete tasks of emancipation (as tends to be true of classical and neo-orthodox theologies) or else (as in the more liberal and postliberal theologies) they speak of emancipation itself in purely abstract terms, ignoring the basic inequalities between different classes and societies and the radically conflictive character of our actual, concrete history.

Thus a constant theme in all the theologies of liberation that are at all methodologically self-conscious is the need for "the liberation of theology," by which they mean the emancipation of theology itself from any such ideological function or misuse. This emancipation can be effected, they urge, only insofar as the prior option and commitment from which theology is done are not simply a believing acceptance of the Christian witness, or even that together with a commitment to secularity, but also a real and effective solidarity with the oppressed, whether they be exploited nations and classes, despised cultures, or discriminated races and sexes. Only when theology is a reflection in and on the actual praxis of emancipation from these kinds of structural bondage — or, in other words, only when theology is a rationalization of just such liberating praxis — can it itself be freed from either being a mere ideology or being misused as one.

From my standpoint, this proposal for the liberation of theology is not really anything of the kind. It is simply one more proposal for the bondage of theology, because on it, no less than on all the earlier understandings, theology remains the rationalization of certain positions instead of being critical reflection on their meaning and truth. It is true that the terms of the bondage are different; and, assuming, as I have argued, that existence in faith is existence for the freedom of others, and so participation in God's emancipating as well as redeeming work, one might well prefer bondage on these terms to any others. But bondage it nonetheless is, and if theology otherwise is open to the charge of ideology, this charge is hardly rendered groundless simply because the positions theology rationalizes are those of the oppressed instead of the oppressors. Indeed, the endemic danger of any such theology is that it will finally be little more than the rationalization of these positions, since it is solely in terms of them that it rationalizes the positions of the Christian witness of faith. Thus, according to one liberation theologian, "Christians should not redefine social praxis by starting with the gospel message. They should do just the opposite. They should seek out the historical import of the gospel by starting with social praxis."[5] That the motives behind such a statement may be of the best, or that one may even share the same social and political sympathies as the person making it, ought not to obscure the fact that the one-sided method it recommends could no more be accepted by an adequate Christian theology than the one-sided method it opposes.

Consequently, my own proposal for the emancipation of theology is quite different. Because the real root of theology's historic bondage is the underlying conception of its task as, in effect, the rationalization of positions already taken, the only way in which it can be emancipated is by reconceiving its task, instead, as critical reflection on such positions. Only insofar as theology is consistently conceived as such reflection — on the positions taken in normative Christian witness as well as on those taken by men and women today in their actual conflictive history — can it be said that theology really is free.

Of course, in order to be such critical reflection, theology has to be governed by certain criteria. But as difficult as it may be to specify just what theology's criteria require in a given situation, there surely can

5. J. P. Richard; quoted in Juan Luis Segundo, S. J., *The Liberation of Theology*, trans. John Drury (Maryknoll, N.Y.: Orbis Books, 1976), p. 85.

be little question about the criteria themselves. They are the very same criteria of appropriateness and credibility that I have spoken of all along. Theology can judge no position to be adequate that is not at once appropriate to the Christian witness as judged by its apostolic norm and credible to human existence as judged in terms of common experience and reason. Because these criteria are not in serious question, there is no reason to doubt that theology not only must but also can be freed from its historic bondage. For if these criteria are a *necessary* condition of theology's being critical reflection instead of mere rationalization, they are also a *sufficient* condition, in that the emancipation of theology can always be effected, provided only that it reflect on all positions in terms of these criteria, and judge no position to be adequate unless it satisfies the requirements of both of them.

The point in urging this proposal, naturally, is in no way to suggest that theology itself ought not to take any positions. The idea of a theology that would be neutral in this sense is absurd. But far from absurd is the idea of a theology that would take the positions it takes on the basis of a critical reflection governed by the two criteria of appropriateness and credibility. In fact, I am quite convinced that this is the only idea of theology as itself radically free, in the twofold sense of being free *for* all positions precisely because it is also free *from* all positions.

The clear implication of this idea, however, is that the only way in which theology as such can be of service to any emancipating praxis is by critically reflecting on its positions in terms of these same criteria. While theological reflection is always free to *result* in positions reflecting the closest solidarity with the oppressed over against their oppressors, it is not in this solidarity, or in the praxis expressive of it, that theology *originates*. On the contrary, the prior option and commitment from which theology springs are simply the prior option and commitment of any and all critical reflection — namely, human existence as such in its profound exigency for the truth that alone can make us free. It is because theology as such exists, above all, to respond to this deep human need for truth that its service to the praxis of emancipation can be only the *indirect* service of critically reflecting on the positions that such praxis implies. The whole point on which I have been insisting, however, is that this is the only service that a truly free theology is in a position to perform.

There will be some, I am sure, for whom this conclusion provokes the question whether the emancipation of theology for which I am calling is, after all, a good thing. But once this question is clearly raised, there can be little doubt about the answer. Whatever else theology may be said to be from the standpoint of Christian faith and witness, it is itself one of the ways in which we as Christians are called to bear witness to our faith — not only by *what* we think and say theologically but also, and no less importantly, by *how* we think and say it. Thus not the least way of attesting one's belief that we are saved, not by our own good works, but solely by the grace of God accepted in faith is to be willing to subject all of one's positions, *including this very belief*, to critical reflection, thereby acknowledging that they are, at best, but our own intellectual good works. To become clear about this, however, is to realize that any theology other than one that is itself genuinely free can hardly bear witness to a God whose gift and demand are radical freedom. Indeed, there must be something strangely contradictory about a theology that explicitly talks about liberation only in such a way as to implicitly attest to its own bondage.

Accordingly, not the least important step we have to take if we would really move toward a theology of liberation is to emancipate theology from its historic bondage as mere rationalization to its proper freedom as critical reflection. To stop short of such emancipation would be to settle for a theology that could not possibly be an adequate theology of liberation, for it could do justice neither to the deep human aspiration to be free nor to the witness of faith that promises to satisfy this aspiration.